# TRUE HELM

# True Helm

A Practical Guide to Northern Warriorship

by

**Sweyn Plowright**

Organiser, Rune-Net

Illustrated

by

**Mark Morte**

ISBN 978-1-4477-7290-3

RUNE-NET PRESS

© 2011

Copyright © 2011
by Sweyn Plowright

First published in 2000

All rights reserved. No part of this book, either in part or in whole may be reproduced transmitted or utilised in any form or by any means electronic, photographic or mechanical, including photocopying, recording, or by any information storage and retrieval system, without the permission in writing from the Publisher, except for brief quotations embodied in literary articles and reviews.

For permissions, write to the Publisher at the address below.

Published by MacKaos Consulting for

Rune-Net Press
sweyn@ mensa.org.au

## ACKNOWLEDGMENTS

This concept was inspired in part by James Chisholm's "True Hearth", and also the encouragement of Geirr Fokstuen. Thanks especially for the support of wife Kara, and friends in Rune-Net.

## DEDICATION

To all who have risked life or reputation to stand against ignorance or tyranny. To name a few: Pythagoras, Egil, Raudh, N.Copernicus, F.Bacon, G.Bruno, H.Abiff, I.Newton, C.Darwin, and the legions who have kept us free by prizing honour and virtue.

## EDITION

This edition is a reprint of the edition published in 2000. Readers requested as few changes as possible. The text and artwork has been faithfully reproduced, warts and all. Despite the temptation to rewrite sections, only outdated information has been changed.

Chisholm's *True Hearth* is available from Amazon:
ISBN 1-447772-90-3

# Contents

## Part I: True Helm

| | |
|---|---|
| Foreword by Ian Read | vi |
| Chapter One - Some Background | 1 |
| Chapter Two - A Little History | 6 |
| Chapter Three - Wyrd Ideas | 13 |
| Chapter Four - Cultivating Hamingja | 18 |
| Chapter Five - Will, Önd, and Fear | 24 |
| Chapter Six - Oaths and Personal Power | 29 |
| Chapter Seven - Sigrunes and Helm of Awe | 34 |
| Chapter Eight - Magickal Weapons | 45 |
| Chapter Nine - Games and Action | 50 |
| Chapter Ten - Principles of Success | 55 |
| Chapter Eleven - Berserker | 59 |
| Chapter Twelve - Justice and Revenge | 63 |
| Chapter Thirteen - Warriorship and Paradox | 67 |

## Part II: Revenge of the Master Smith

| | |
|---|---|
| Revenge of the Master Smith | 71 |
| Enter The Skald | 75 |
| Chapter One - King Wada's Hall | 77 |
| Chapter Two - The Journey | 83 |
| Chapter Three - The Trollman | 89 |
| Chapter Four - The Nomads | 95 |
| Chapter Five - The Yrminsul | 103 |
| Chapter Six - Wolfdales | 109 |
| Chapter Seven - King Nidhad's Hall | 115 |
| Chapter Eight - Massacre at Wolfdales | 121 |
| Chapter Nine - The Valkyries | 125 |
| Chapter Ten - The Curse | 131 |
| Chapter Eleven - The Prisoner | 137 |
| Chapter Twelve - Saevarstead | 143 |
| Chapter Thirteen - Revenge | 147 |
| Exit the Skald | 153 |
| Further Reading | 155 |

# Foreword

Senior managers have for some time now been aware of the knowledge to be gleaned from such guides to the tactics and philosophy of fighting as Musashi's *The Book of Five Rings*, Sun Tzu's *The Art of War*, and others. This book is the Germanic equivalent to these masterpieces, encoding as it does this ancient tradition's answers to such perennial questions as 'How do I defend myself safely and legally in this modern world?' and 'How may I live as a warrior without behaving anachronistically?' The word encoded is used here deliberately because Sweyn does precisely this, he hides sacred and holy wisdom in plain view.

When studying works on the ancient wisdom one may rightly ask how the author one reads is qualified to write about this area. In Sweyn's case the answer is at least two-fold. Firstly, he qualifies because of his long background in the Martial Arts, his time in the British Army and because (as I can personally attest) he is a man who will stand shoulder to shoulder in the shield-wall and never leave it until victory or death ensues. This point may sound somewhat corny in this modern, 'hip' age but is nevertheless good enough grounds to accord honour to the one it is said about. Which leads me to the second reason: honour. Our Germanic system has much to say about honour as it is in many ways the linchpin around which the True man revolves. Such a man has powerful Truths to cast forth into the multiverse and such a man is Sweyn.

Study and live by this book's guidelines and you may create such a strong inner being (that we call *hamingja*) and may even, upon death, join those greatest of all warriors, the *Einherjar* who fight for Óðhinn in Valhalla.

Ian Read
Master and Hall Leader of Eormensyl Hall, London.

*One should never be far from one's weapons*
*When faring from home*
*You can never be certain when you will need*
*The use of your spear while out and about* [1]

*The Helm of Awe hides no one*
*When warriors draw their swords*
*When many meet to test their strength*
*They will find none is foremost* [2]

Our Germanic ancestors put great value on warriorship, and also on the creative and poetic use of words. Often words with more than one meaning were used to enrich a phrase, deliberately introducing ambiguity to convey multiple levels of meaning. It is in this tradition that I have chosen the word 'helm'.

On one hand, the helm is the controlling point of the ship. On the other, the helm is the house of the head, bearing the crest in battle, providing protection and projecting intent. The True Helm is the Helm of Awe, whose hallowed and mythological origin is in the treasure hoard of the Volsungs [3]. This is a symbol of the warrior spirit. The Helm of Awe also describes a uniquely Germanic magickal technique which I will discuss later.

---

[1] From the Hávamál verse 38, my translation
[2] From Fáfnismál verse 17, Transl L Hollander
[3] See Saga of the Volsungs, Transl J Byock

Warriorship is a personal and individual path. It is a path which deals with all aspects of life. The essence of warriorship is the process of fulfilling one's potential. The ways toward warriorship are many, and they are all hard. Few ever go far, though all benefit. This is a commitment to a life of discipline and development in mind, body, and soul. The true warrior is an athlete, a scholar, a poet, a magician, a priest, and a skilled lover.

This book is not intended to be a rigorous academic tome, although I try to utilise the most reputable sources to gain a picture of our pre-Kristjan[4] heritage. In this book I hope to offer an approach to Northern spiritual warriorship, and provide some useful advice for those on this demanding path.

As this is such a personal path, I feel that I must at this point share an outline of my own experience which has led me to write this book. This may be useful to some readers to gain insights, but others may wish to skip this and go on to the next chapter.

I have had a fortunate start, being an Australian, of Dutch and Danelaw-English parentage, born into an Air Force family. I was well travelled at an early age and received no religious indoctrination. I was a sceptic with an interest in the sciences from about the age of seven.

My first martial arts were Judo at age ten, and due to yet another move, Tae Kwon Do at eleven. At twelve I was awakened to the Runes after reading JRR Tolkien's books. The year was 1972 ev. My interest in Germanic magick and religion continued to grow despite my scepticism. For the next four years, I sought out academic information on runology. I also became proficient at archery, competing at a local level.

At sixteen, I started regular meditation and a conscious commitment to the way of Odin. At eighteen, I commenced studies in physics and maths at university. I also took up Kung Fu and joined the university weightlifting team.

---

[4] An Old Norse spelling of 'Christian'

Toward the end of my second year at university, I had two runic experiences which shook my scepticism and forced me to accept that rune magick is more than an intellectual game.

In 1979 ev I had a room on campus. One rainy weekend I decided to make a Thor's hammer to hang on my door. I cut it out of thick card and decorated it with knotwork and runes. I finished it with the focused intent of warding the door. I pinned it to the door and thought no more about it. Despite the feeling of intense seriousness, almost reverence, I felt for the hammer making, my rational mind explained the exercise as a bonding with my ancestral culture. I was a science student after all.

Half an hour later, I avoided studying by deciding to wash my growing pile of dirty clothes. There were about six floors in the building, each with a small laundry with two washing machines. Finding a queue at the laundry on my floor, I went upstairs to find their laundry deserted. Both machines were running, one was just finishing. I took the freshly washed clothes out of the finished machine and put them in the nearby basket.

On checking that the machine was empty, I found a room key in it. I checked the number engraved on it so I could return it, but it had my room number. I thought I must have dropped my key in the machine while leaning over it, but my key was still in my pocket. The hair started to rise on the back of my neck.

After loading my washing and starting the machine, I went back to my room to test the key in my lock. It was indeed a copy of my room key. I went straight back up to see if I could work out who had a copy of my key in their washing. When I arrived, their washing was gone. I never discovered who it was or why.

If I had gone to the laundry downstairs, or gone a few minutes later, someone would have had easy access to my room. The probability of being in that place at exactly that time was exceedingly small. This was a powerful demonstration of the working of the Germanic concept of wyrd, which I will discuss later.

The second incident was an even more direct experience although not as 'weird/wyrd'. I arose one morning to find my motorcycle missing. After notifying the Police and getting an increasing picture of hopelessness, I felt a distinct bloodlust rising.

I took a bus to my parent's house and started to play some Wagner very loud on the stereo. The folks were out at work at that time. I let the rage rise with the volume of the music. I visualised being a wolf and chasing down my enemy to tear at his throat.

As if in answer, the wind rose sweeping dark clouds to blot out the bright sunlight. A sudden autumn squall blew in from the nearby mountains, not unusual at that time of year. After about ten minutes of fury, horizontal rain, and tiles flying off rooftops, the storm subsided and the afternoon sun returned. I felt much calmer and able to accept the fate of my bike.

Half an hour later, the Police phoned. The motorbike was found blown off the road. The thief would have been injured in the fall, but the bike ended up relatively unscathed in a muddy ditch.

Although my rational side kept saying "coincidence", I started to feel a need to search for my ancestral roots in Europe. I went to England and joined the British Army. I visited the ancient sites, and saw active service. I did not find what I thought I had been looking for, but gained something more valuable. The discipline I had learned opened the way to my next stage of learning.

At twenty three, I returned to university to study psychology and linguistics. There I met a fellow psych student with a sinister reputation as a magician. A powerful looking Norwegian gentleman fifteen years my senior, he inspired a cautious approach. After getting to know him as a friend, and discovering his deep commitment to his martial arts and the Odinic path, I became a student of his combat style.

In 1988 ev I wrote to Edred Thorsson, and established the Rune-Gild, South Pacific Region. I have organised yearly Gild feasts, and continued my study in runes, warriorship, and practical combat. I have also visited Gild members in London and in Woodharrow, Texas.

During a visit to Woodharrow I was inspired to write this book. I was moved by James Chisholm's passion and commitment, and the music of Ian Read, comrade in arms of my London stay three years earlier, who presented his Gild Master-work, the music CD 'Rûna' at that gathering.

Chisholm's book 'True Hearth' outlines the way of the Northern Heathen household. I have designed this book to complement it as much as possible it in style and content.

I recently left the Rune-Gild following an almost unanimous vote by the membership of the South Pacific Region to become an independent, more web-based, rune-study network, Rune-Net.

I currently work as a computer network engineer in a large computer corporation. I have constructed a public Rune-Net web site at ...

http://www.mackaos.com.au/Rune-Net

also a web site for Rune-Net members only.

*Wits are needed by those who travel far,*
*Anything goes at home,*
*But ignorance will make one a laughing stock,*
*When seated among the wise* [5]

*A house is better, though small it may be*
*One is somebody at home*
*Two goats and a thatched cottage*
*Are still much better than begging* [6]

The earliest significant written records describing our Germanic ancestors are the writings of the Roman scholar Tacitus. He describes them as fierce and independent people, loyal to kin and comrades. Favoured weapons were sword and axe, and even more so, shield and spear. This may have been the origin of the name 'ger-man' men of the spear.

Tacitus wrote the *Germania* in the year 98 ce. He speaks with obvious admiration about the many tribes north of the Rhine. The tribes varied in custom, but had mutually intelligible dialects. It was primarily by this recognisable unity of language that Tacitus classifies these tribes as 'German'. They valued courage and fought in relatively small groups, usually of kin, following a chief. Loyalty to a chief was what held the warrior band together and gave the warriors a focus beyond themselves.

---

[5] From the Hávamál verse 5, my translation
[6] From the Hávamál verse 36, my translation

Gifts were given freely, and hospitality was an accepted norm of their society. Women were honoured and often accompanied their kinsmen close behind the battle lines. Dowries were given by husbands to their brides, and women were always consulted before a battle.

Freedom was an essential feature of early Germanic society. Laws were simple and designed to place responsibility for actions on the individual. The laws were often flexible in their implementation. It was common to settle blood feuds with payment of cattle and goods to avoid excessive bloodshed. In most tribes, the wearing of weapons was universal. In some, youths would be required to train in weapons skills and discipline before being allowed to bear arms in public.

Gambling with dice was a serious business and debts were discharged as a matter of honour, even if it meant selling oneself into slavery. Luck, courage, and honour were inseparable concepts.

Several centuries later we can see the same virtues extolled in the early Anglo-Saxon poetry. Favourite themes are the exploits of heroes, both home grown and from the ancestral lands of the continent. Stories of strength, courage, and most of all loyalty, are framed in powerful and moving verse. These poems come from an ancient oral tradition linguistically distinct from the prose of the time.

Often the *wyrd* of a warrior is mentioned in a sense somewhere between fate, luck, and personal power.

The Vikings were the last, and perhaps best known, of the heathen Germanic peoples. Much has been written about them by their contemporaries and by chroniclers not long after. The rich literary tradition of the sagas gives us a valuable insight into the Viking world. Many of the features of Viking life can be seen to be inherited from earlier times.

As in most Germanic tribes before, the Vikings were usually not professional soldiers, but were well armed and skilful warriors in a dangerous world. Whatever their civilian occupations, most Viking males were required to be able to defend themselves with deadly force. Many were opportunistic and went on raiding parties for gain and glory. Most warfare took place between Viking groups, or with their Germanic neighbours.

Women generally presided over the home and hearth, but there are rare reports of women choosing a path of arms. Nonetheless, they were tough and able, and often played decisive roles in the sagas. The concept of women taking the path of warriorship was not at all alien to the Germanic peoples; the image of the Valkyrie certainly conveys the idea of warrior women.

Also in common with their ancestors, Vikings went in small groups loyal to a leader. A chief had a *hirð*, a group of warriors whose number depended on the chief's status and wealth. A group of warriors sworn to a common loyalty or purpose was termed a *felag*. This translates as 'fee-lay', indicating that these partnerships were often seen as commercial ventures. The oaths of loyalty involved in such a venture were still taken very seriously. The word *felag* has come down to us as 'fellow' and the idea of fellowship.

The common threads running through all of these sources are the power of the individual and the joy of loyalty to a worthy lord or fellowship. Idealistic causes would have been seen as shallow, pointless, even frivolous reasons to fight, but blood is the bond and only for blood should blood be spilled. Blood brotherhood demanded as strong a loyalty as kinship.

With the coming of the Kristjan era, our culture became increasingly hidden and was almost forgotten. Thanks to the dedicated few, enough has been preserved or revived to give us a fairly accurate body of lore with which to bring our true culture back to life in a form which is both authentic in substance and effective in the modern world.

The importance of reliable sources cannot be stressed enough. Our culture cannot be reclaimed without a solid foundation in fact. We are fortunate to have access to a large archive of reputable material. We must use this resource in an inspired but disciplined manner to extract the value of our inheritance. Let us learn from the many fantasy 'traditions' around us who claim a long European heritage, but are manifestly recent inventions designed to cater to the longing for heritage which many feel in an acculturated society.

Just take a walk through an occult bookstore and see how many authors try to pass off a hotch potch of Eastern and Judaic mysticism as a European tradition. One would think that we never had our own culture, or that it was something to be ashamed of.

Perhaps the best and biggest example of misrepresentation in this genre is the phenomenon of 'Wicca'. Although it has many admirable features, and its members are genuine, its adherents often claim a European, usually Celtic, heritage dating from the Middle Ages or even Neolithic times, depending on who you talk to. It is presented as an ancient form of European Duotheism, and affectionately known as 'the Old Religion'.

A little research, however, reveals several inconsistencies. Firstly the name 'Wicca' pronounced 'wikka', claimed to mean 'craft of the wise', can only be found in an Old English Dictionary and is actually the masculine form of the noun 'witch' and was pronounced 'witcha'. The word is not found in any Celtic language but is Germanic (Anglo-Saxon). Although most of their seasonal celebrations have Celtic names, they celebrate 'Yule', another very Germanic word. We could give them the benefit of the doubt and assume word borrowing some time in history, but it gets worse.

Nearly all of the sources cited in Wiccan books can be traced back to four books popular in the first half of the twentieth century: Frazer's *Golden Bough*, Murray's *The Witch-Cult in Western Europe*, Graves' *The White Goddess*, and Leland's *Aradia*. All of these books have been discredited as either romantic and inaccurate, or outright invention.

Without too much detective work, it soon becomes obvious that not so long ago, within living memory (late 1940s), Gerald Gardner cobbled together ideas from the four books plus Inquisition witch confessions, added some of his own knowledge of Malay magic and Golden Dawn[7] magic, threw in some folklore, and with some help from the poetic genius of Aleister Crowley, Wicca was born.

A linguistic analysis of the Wiccan 'Book of Shadows' confirms its recent origin. An anthropological analysis of the Wiccan system and its underlying assumptions also reveals a post-Kristjan origin. No evidence for anything like it can be found in pre-Kristjan Europe.

But the debunking of Wicca is certainly not my intention. I have included this short summary merely as a warning. Unless we all become scholars in our own heritage, we stand to lose it to fantasy 'traditions'. While there is nothing wrong with inventing new systems, most of those interested in the Northern path are attempting to forge a genuine link with their ancestors, and with the power of that heritage.

Perhaps the greatest obstacle we face is the prejudice aroused by the Nazi abuse of Germanic culture. Nazi propaganda used the heroic Germanic history and legend to inspire their followers and justify their excesses. It is now difficult to separate Germanic pride from Nazism in the minds of many, even for some within Ásatrú. It may be useful to know, however, that despite his use of Heathen symbolism, Hitler introduced the Kristjan Church Tax and continued to pay it until his death. The stereotype of the Macho-Viking-Nazi will haunt us for some time to come, but good scholarship will ultimately win out. We will need the skills of warriorship to survive the challenge of reclaiming our heritage. Focus, determination, and strategy will decide the outcome.

In a multi-cultural society I have often been described by the establishment as 'non-ethnic', confirming the perception that our people are cultureless. Let us look at the Native American example. There has been an active movement in recent decades for these people to reclaim their heritage. They too have a warrior tradition, and share many attitudes with us. They have publicly applauded the Ásatrú movement for providing our people with its own culture, and are sick and tired of seeing

---

[7] An occult order founded in the 19th century by English Freemasons

buckskin-wearing pseudo-medicine-men with no Native American connection other than some New Age books by other pseudo-medicine-men.

The Native Americans rightly feel insulted at their culture being prostituted and devalued. While it is one thing (and rare) to be genuinely adopted and initiated into another culture, it is quite another to assume the trappings of a culture without that deep connection. They find it hard to understand why people seek for cultural roots anywhere but in their own ancestry.

To those who think that reclaiming their cultural heritage implies prejudice against others, I can definitely say that the truth is quite the opposite. In my experience, and that of others on our path, there is a greater ease, respect, and understanding between Asatruar and those of other traditional cultures than most modern westerners ever experience.

It is now called 'political correctness' to be supportive of an individual's ethnic pride, we should expect no less consideration for our own.

We should also think about the future of our people in terms of past trends. The history of our ancestors has been, from the beginning, one of expansion and colonisation. While we look to Scandinavia as our spiritual birthplace (Tacitus called it the Womb of Nations), the most dynamic expression of our heritage has always been on the frontiers. It is only through feedback from the frontiers that the centre can be rejuvenated. If our culture ceases to push into new frontiers, it will fall into stagnation and decrepitude, like so many great civilisations have in the past.

The last great expansions of our people, into America and Australia, have now come to a halt, maturing into stable nationhood. It is fortunate that just as we have run out of options for expansion on Earth, technology has put other worlds within reach. It would be easy to bury our heads in the sand at home, and cling to one fragile piece of rock, but it has never been our way to refuse a challenge. We need to start thinking now about the future of our culture in the next phase of expansion, which is only two or three generations away at most.

The greatest obstacle to our success is the 1967 Outer Space Treaty, originally designed to prevent confrontations between the two space powers at that time, the USA and USSR, which prohibits ownership of land away from Earth by any government, company, or individual. This treaty effectively also prohibits the establishment of law in any colony. I do not think the treaty will be much of an obstacle in practice. Laws which would have made the colonisation of Iceland or America difficult were soon overturned in the face of the evolving situation. As with any colony, self rule is only a matter of time.

Some readers will be uncomfortable contemplating the future, being more accustomed to focusing on the past 2000 years, but unless we give an equal eye to the next millennium, the heroic deeds of our ancestors will have been for nothing. Perhaps Wyrd was speaking when they named the first Mars lander "Viking".

*There are many good omens, if one knew*
*When swords start flashing*
*For a warrior to be followed*
*By a raven so black* [8]

*Words now are chanted, on the Sage's seat,*
*At the Well of Wyrd*
*I saw and was silent, I saw and thought,*
*I listened to human speech*
*I heard of runes and their portents, and interpretations announced,*
*At the High One's Hall*
*In the High One's Hall*
*I heard it said so:* [9]

An essential part of the Germanic world view was the concept of *wyrd*. Underlying all events and manifest in every shape, *wyrd* is present.

The word 'wyrd' is Anglo-Saxon meaning 'coming into being', and is cognate with the German *verden*. The word also had a much deeper meaning implying the unseen forces which influence the coming into being. Upon seeing an omen, one might say "that is wyrd". Eventually much of the meaning was lost and we now have 'weird', meaning merely 'strange' or 'supernatural'.

---

[8] From the Reginsmal verse 20, my translation
[9] Hávamál verse 111, my translation

Many of the old poems speak of a warrior's wyrd. Translators usually equate this with 'fate'. A study of the literature reveals, however, that wyrd was a much more sophisticated concept than the Kristjan idea of divinely planned and immutable destiny.

Some equate 'wyrd' with 'karma'. Although in the more enlightened traditions, karma is merely the law of cause and effect, most have a connotation of divine retribution, a moralistic payback system. Our understanding of wyrd goes beyond shortsighted human morality, and even beyond causality as it is normally understood. Wyrd is best understood as the seen and unseen relationships of the individual consciousness with the world and its events.

Wyrd is represented by a tapestry woven by the three Norns. The Norns weave blindly according to the necessities of natural law, *Ørløg*. The word *Ørløg* means 'primal law' and is the most fundamental layer of the structure of the multiverse. Even the gods cannot escape their wyrd, which is wrought by the interaction of their words and deeds with Ørløg. Thus for us, there is no need for a supreme being as understood by Kristjans, although one is free to see Ørløg as an expression of the multiverse as a supreme being. The essential concept here is that every individual consciousness is responsible for its own wyrd.

The three Norns make an appearance in Shakespeare's *Macbeth* as the Weird Sisters. The point of the tale is often misunderstood. The Norns reveal some predictions to Macbeth. He then makes decisions which lead to the fulfilment of the Norns' prophesy. It is clear that only through his own choices does Macbeth bring about the events foreseen by the Norns. The events become inevitable only because of Macbeth's decisions to act on the prophesies, not because they were pre-ordained.

The importance of the Norns in the Odinic world view is seldom appreciated by historians and mythologers. Most commonly they are merely equated to the Greek Fates (Past, Present, and Future). Although the two trios of weavers undoubtedly stem from the same mythological source, the concepts which they represent are subtly different.

If we look at the names of the three Norns (Urd, Skuld, and Verdandi) and their mythological context, we can go a long way toward grasping the concepts they embody.

'Urd' is cognate with 'Wyrd', the Anglo-Saxon word for the unseen influences behind events. It also suggests the primal or ancient. Urd is depicted as being the guardian of a bottomless well. Urd's well is the primal source and Urd represents the unmanifest potential, everything arises from the unmanifest and returns to it. All possibilities exist therein.

'Skuld' translates directly as 'should'. This is because Skuld represents that which can be inferred. Given the present indications we can predict what *should* happen, but we can take steps to avert the outcome. If there is free will, no system of prediction can be foolproof. Hence we have 'Should' and not 'Shall'. There is also the implication of debt, which may or may not be paid, but *should* if all progresses without interference and with honour.

'Verdandi' denotes that which is becoming or manifesting, the present moment. Verdandi represents the dynamic process of 'coming into being' which we perceive as the manifest world.

Skuld can also include 'that which should have been', so that the manifest decays back through Skuld to return to the unmanifest. We can see that rather than simply having a representation of linear time, we have a concept of all things being in a state of change.

To our perception, there are three realms of Wyrd: That which we cannot perceive, Urd; that which we perceive directly, Verdandi; and that which we can infer by logic or by divination, Skuld. All things exist within the Wyrd and are interconnected by it, hence the symbolism of a web or woven strands. Everything has its effect on everything else. Our Wyrd is a web of interconnections within a larger web. Working our True Will requires the ability to move with freedom within the constraints of our Wyrd, bearing in mind that our every action changes our Wyrd. By understanding the Norns, we can come to understand our Wyrd.

This concept is a vital part of our system, and it comes into play in all of our work from Rune Magick to martial training. In our system, we relate Urd to meditation. In meditation we look deep into the well of the unmanifest within, when thought stops we can perceive our connection with the Wyrd, this is the source of our True Will, our individuality and real power.

Skuld relates to active training, where skills are honed but situations are hypothetical. Our actions in the world at large are in the realm of Verdandi, where we are fully in the present and acting without hesitation. A Master remains in all three realms simultaneously.

The Norns and the Wyrd are a ubiquitous background upon which we interact with the Gods, and to which even the Gods are subject. It is perhaps this background nature which makes us tend to take them for granted.

Wyrd has a quality of paradox and poetry, and was often a feature of traditional Germanic tales. Oaths also play a large role. The intertwining of word and wyrd is symbolised by the oath ring. The personal power, wyrd, and luck of the individual can be destroyed by the breaking of an oath. A well made oath empowers the individual.

It is in this sense that the Hávamál states that 'a gift demands a gift'[10]. It is not a matter of debt. Giving freely, without expectation, was an important feature of our culture noted by Tacitus and later writers. The return is in the empowerment of wyrd by the act of giving freely, from a sense of appropriateness. Giving with the intention to create debt will backfire. Thus it is also written 'better there be no prayer than excessive sacrifice'[11].

---

[10] Hávamál verses 42, 46, and 145
[11] Hávamál verse 145

The practices of generosity and hospitality are not easy to cultivate in this age of treachery and mistrust. The virtues valued by our ancestors must be practised in an environment compatible with theirs. This is the purpose of the True Hearth: find others with honour and troth with whom to practise. Your kindred are of vital importance to your wyrd.

Your wyrd will be enhanced by an awareness of the quality of the kinfolk beside you and the ancestors behind you. They form a vital part of the tradition, and the power of the tradition. This power is ours to benefit from, and ours to protect.

## 4

*Only the mind knows what is near to the heart*
*And alone sees what it feels*
*There is no worse illness, wise men know*
*Than not to be content with anything* [12]

The process of cultivating a warrior's wyrd involves developing the focused magickal will and its manifestation, the *hamingja*. The building of the *hamingja* is the discipline of warriorship. Just as a genuine tradition relies on a solid foundation of knowledge, a powerful *hamingja* relies on a solid foundation of inner discipline.

Our tradition has always recognised that the human mind/body complex consists of many selves. Although these selves are interconnected, they also have a measure of independence. Thus it is possible, even likely, that the forces of self contradict each other much of the time.

It is the Kristjan simplification of soul/body duality which is responsible for much of the ego sickness of the modern world. We are led to believe that we consist of a body controlled by a single soul (mind, personality, or ego). We suffer the illusion that when each of our conflicting selves takes control, we are merely changing moods. This is the reason for the schizoid and confused state of the average citizen.

---

[12] Hávamál verse 95, my translation

Only when the true nature of the mind/body complex is understood can we hope to gain some control of our minds and bodies. Only by becoming aware of the constant chatter and turmoil in our minds can we start to do something to make our minds useful. By training our divided selves to work together, we can work toward realising our potential.

Most people go through life never knowing what they really want. Society's values, peer pressure, and advertising all instil false desires which convince us that we must have certain things to be happy. Once we have these things, we are still not satisfied. In such a state, the manifestation of will is weakened and the false desires work against it.

Only by regularly silencing the competing minds within can we become aware of our true desires. These directions will lead to a sense of fulfilment. Meditation is the key to achieving this silence.

The practice of meditation is ancient and almost universal. While techniques vary between places and times, the aim is always the same: awareness without thought. Unfortunately, this useful and well defined word has been so loosely used by charlatans and New Agers in recent times that it has almost lost all meaning. It is often used to refer to visualisation, path working, contemplation, and many other mind exercises. I propose that meditation is such a unique and powerful tool that we should be strict in the use of the term.

Any technique of meditation will involve focusing the mind to a single thought until even that thought can be let go. The result is clarity of mind and an awareness free of the learned responses, judgements, and preconceptions which hide true experience from us. In this state, the power and direction of the Will can be sensed directly.

### Isa Rune Meditation Technique:

Choose a time when your stomach is not full and you are not too tired, before breakfast and dinner are best. Sit in a straight backed chair preferably with the head unsupported. Set a timer for 15 to 20 minutes and sit in an upright but relaxed position with the eyes lightly closed.

Start by visualising an icicle, focus on the stillness of ice. After a couple of minutes you should have replaced the mind's turmoil with this one image. Now you can start the actual meditation and let the image go.

Repeat the sound "i" (the sound of the vowel in 'hit') in the mind and carefully observe how it develops from a thought into the imagined sound. At this stage unwanted thoughts will interfere, just bring the mind gently back to the repeating "i". Eventually the unwanted thoughts will die down and the thought of the "i" sound will have replaced the sound itself.

Carefully observe what is causing the repeating thought of the sound of "i". Note that you must not think of these observations as questions, this would merely result in diverting the mind to the thought of the question and on to other questions; the meditation would be right off the track in seconds.

Merely observe the thought of the "i" mantra to discover its source. When you discover the origin of the thought, this impulse will replace the thought. Observe the impulse which starts the thought which creates the sound of "i" in the mind. At this stage the "i" and even the thought of it will have disappeared and there will be only a subtle repeating pulse.

Usually after a couple of months of daily practice it is possible to follow the pulse back to its origin. This is what we call the Region of Pure Will. You will suddenly find that you have been utterly devoid of thought for an unknown length of time. After a couple of years of practice it is possible to remain in this state for most of the meditation. At this stage you will experience the Region of Pure Will as a place of utter calm yet immense power; this is your True Self.

Note that you will be fully aware and present at all stages. If you find yourself going off with the fairies, or indulging in some technicolour light show in your head, just gently return to the mantra. If you start falling asleep, go to bed, or try again when more awake.

When the timer goes off let the mind do as it will and slowly return to your normal state. Stretch and open the eyes. You will notice the benefits of this practice in all areas of your life within a few months of starting.

In the longer term, this method will allow glimpses of states of extreme clarity, and shifts of perspective which show the inadequacy of every-day three dimensional logic. The only way to illustrate the effect is by analogy.

Imagine a planet covered in a vast plane of volcanic glass, perfectly smooth and flat. It rotates so that the same side always faces its sun, and the atmosphere is humid and still with no clouds. The beings who evolve there are flat and circular, sliding across the smooth plane. Their vision is adapted to see only a thin horizontal strip. They understand the horizontal directions, but have no concept of up or down.

Their houses are just walls, of normal thickness, but almost no height. A roof is not only unnecessary, but not even a possible concept. They feel quite secure in these houses as they can not see through the walls, are physically incapable of entering without using a door.

All they could see of us is the side of the sole of our shoe. If we lift our foot, we would seem to vanish, and magically appear somewhere else. We can stand outside a house and still see in. By stepping over a wall, we can vanish and appear inside a locked room.

How could we explain to them what we are doing, or how we see? Flat logic dictates that what is behind a wall is not visible. Inside and outside are mutually exclusive, one cannot be both at the same time. Yet from above, we can. Our explanations would only seem self contradictory and illogical to them.

In much the same way, many of the world's mystical writings appear in some ways similar, and in other ways contradictory. After glimpsing some of the perspective shifts, it soon becomes clear that the contradictions are the failure of the language of ordinary awareness to cope with mystical states. Many of the conflicts between religious views are based entirely upon dogmas resulting from different ways of trying to describe something which defies description. Concepts based on these limiting dogmas are of questionable usefulness. Until mystical states are experienced, the usefulness of particular esoteric theories can only be assessed by their practical effects in Midgard, and whether they help us or hinder us in achieving our goals.

Another important part of enhancing our ability to act in the world is the building of a reputation. This has a direct impact on the hamingja and wyrd, and was considered of great importance to our ancestors. As it says in the Hávamál:

Cattle die, Kinfolk die
We will ourselves die also
One thing never dies
A well won reputation [13]

Winning a reputation involves some strategy. In Viking times, great reputations became widely known. Today society takes less notice of individual achievement. For most of us, each time we move to a new job or town, we must re-create our reputation. To some, this offers a second chance.

The only way to create a reputation is to strive to be the best. Having stated the obvious, there are some simple strategies which I have found useful in building a durable and well known reputation.

Start with some modesty. Generating too high an expectation in a new environment is dangerous. Under greater scrutiny and pressure to perform, your first mistake will likely be better remembered than anything else about you. If you start giving the impression of being just a little above average, you will still have some cards up your sleeve. An early mistake will be easily forgotten.

---

[13] Hávamál verse 76, my translation

After building a solid foundation, gradually and almost casually coming out with increasingly impressive surprises, your reputation will become unshakeable. Opportunities will present themselves, and your words and deeds will gain increasing influence upon your wyrd. If such a reputation can be maintained without excessive ego, you are well on the way to a truly powerful hamingja.

Reputation is also directly effected by your peer group or kindred. The power of their reputation and the power of their wyrd will attach itself to your hamingja. Success breeds success, and many organisations recognise the importance of drawing from a tradition of success. In the ideal situation, there is a synergistic effect between the wyrd of the group and the hamingja of the individual, each reinforcing the other.

The ability of wyrd and reputation to flow between associates is a two-edged process. While honourable associates will enhance you, there are some who will only drag you down. It may be difficult to deal with such people because, being an honourable person yourself, you feel that you owe them loyalty for their friendship. This problem is not easily resolved. You may be able to lead by example, or talk them into improving themselves; you may find that you have to just start to distance yourself and gradually let them go their own way. You may have to tell them to get lost.

As you progress along this path, you will find that you will start to attract the right associates. Those who would not be a credit to you will tend to drift away naturally. In the end, it will be up to your conscience when to contribute to a friendship. On the one hand, try not to act for purely selfish reasons; on the other, try not to waste your energy and wyrd on those who are unworthy.

*It is the greatest intimacy to reveal to another
one's whole mind
There is nothing worse than being shallow
It is no friend who never says anything unpleasant* [14]

*A sixth I know: if wounded by one
with a sapling's root,
instead of harming me,
it will eat at the one who tries to harm me* [15]

The body is the primary vehicle/tool/weapon of the warrior. If it is allowed to deteriorate, there will be little hope of fulfilling your potential. Exercise and diet are the keys to maintaining physical health and mental acuity. While the body/mind complex is a collection of different systems, each of these systems effects all of the others. Only by bringing them all into harmony can we create the unity of purpose required to manifest the True Will.

Although each person will have different needs, the initial aim of any health regimen is balance. Start off with light but regular exercise and a diet with a wide variety of food types. Dietary exclusions are not a good idea unless there is a medical reason. Although when a good level of fitness is established, exclusion of an item can be a useful exercise of discipline if not done for more than a couple of months.

---

[14] Hávamál verse 124, my translation
[15] Hávamál verse 151, my translation

Gradually increase the exercise level, including both aerobic and strength exercises. Once at a level of fitness and strength where few tasks will leave you puffing or strained, maintain that level of exercise. There is little to be gained by wasting time and resources maintaining a level of strength or fitness far beyond that which you may need. These levels can be adjusted to cope with increased needs when they arise. Excessive training can cause undue wear on joints which will be regretted later.

It is important to balance both exercise and diet so that all functions are enhanced. This balance is a dynamic equilibrium which will constantly change with the seasons and the activities. After a while you will develop an intuitive feel for the needs and problems of the body. Your body should generally not bring itself to your attention.

If the physical body is neglected, the hamingja will also diminish, and the deficiencies become a distraction. Cultivate awareness of the body's needs. Satisfy them without over-indulging. You will find that there will be an optimum level for all nutrients and activities which will result in fitness, strength, and a feeling of well being.

Beyond mere health, there are more subtle powers available to the body. These will be familiar to some from their Eastern names. Chi and Prana, are probably the most commonly heard terms today. More recent Germanic researchers have used the terms Odic force and Orgone energy. This is an almost universally held belief in a life energy associated with the body, particularly the breath. In the Northern tradition it is called the Önd.

Önd can be visualised as a kind of energy which is absorbed on the in-breath and circulated around the body. At first it will seem that the effect is merely the intake of oxygen, but further practice reveals much more than can be explained so easily.

Exercises to develop awareness and strengthening of Önd involve controlled breathing and visualisation of energy flow. These are usually taught in the context of a martial art. The advantages of controlled breathing include greater mental focus, increased speed, less tendency to tire and, most important, the ability to stay calm in difficult situations. These techniques are best learned from an experienced teacher as the more advanced techniques can do more harm than good if not learned correctly.

If a teacher is not available, find a training partner and practise breathing deeper and slower during exercises and sparring. As a general rule, breathe in sharply while blocking, hold in while delivering a strike, and exhale in a crisp but relaxed manner in the follow-through.

The ideal training partner for energy work is a lover. Learning to move and to feel the body energies with such a degree of intimacy and trust will hasten the learning process considerably. Regular training with others should also be arranged so that you can become accustomed to the substantial differences between individuals.

Training on these levels goes far beyond mere techniques. You will find that you must challenge many fears and hang-ups inherited from our society's past Kristjan domination. To really be in control of a situation, you must become intimate with your opponent (someone you may never have seen before) to a degree which most of us find instinctively uncomfortable. This discomfort is in fact self inflicted, and merely a learned response. Once we learn to be comfortable with the concept, we can become one with our opponents and join them in a joyous, but deadly, dance.

You will learn to quickly get a feel for an opponent's energy and movement. Moving in close to crowd the opponent's actions, you can create the windows of opportunity which allow for unhurried and surgical strikes which finish the matter before you can be struck.

A good knowledge of anatomy is a definite bonus to a warrior, both in targeting strikes, and in first aid should you or your kin be hurt. Learn also not to be upset at the sight of blood. Often a fairly minor wound will produce what looks like a bucketful. If you are unfamiliar with the sight of fresh blood, you will vastly over-estimate the amount lost. Although a severed artery could kill in a few minutes, a moment of panic could leave you exposed to a swifter death when facing an attacker. In practice, most wounds will leave you plenty of time to get to a hospital.

To control the breath, and also the situation, inhale during your opponent's strike. Visualise yourself absorbing the opponent's energy as you deflect the blow. This is easiest to achieve if you use a minimal deflecting force when possible. "A miss is as good as a mile". You only need to prevent the strike from connecting. You do not need to deflect it more than a couple of inches in most cases.

The subtle deflection, or soft block, has two main advantages. Firstly, you will not waste nearly as much energy. Secondly, your opponent will be less able to react off the block with a counter move. This is because the jolt of a hard block will alert the opponent to the move much more quickly. The extra time needed for the opponent's reaction will be a very valuable asset in your defence.

Once you have 'inhaled' your opponent's energy, you can use the brief pause you have created to clear the mind and explode from a totally calm moment. With practise, this happens in an instant, although it will seem that you have plenty of time. The strike will be aimed, surgical, and devastating. Exhale sharply a fraction after contact.

Another advantage of the soft block is that it can be fed smoothly into a twisting or breaking manoeuvre. More importantly, this kind of block allows you to stay in contact with the opponent. By maintaining contact, you can feel for the opponent's intent and react instantly to changes in direction without clashing or being taken by surprise.

Through regular practise, you will come to know the way your body moves best, and the way another body moves. By subtle redirection of movement, you can optimise your position, and with little effort, use your opponent's own motion to cause strain on joints and painful rupture of ligaments and tendons. It is surprising how easy it is to cause an attacker excruciating pain and serious damage merely by helping a limb to continue in the direction which its owner put so much energy into. A punch involves a forceful straightening of the elbow. A tap or tug in the right place and time adds just enough force to the movement to over-straighten the joint. Such an injury would make it impossible for the limb to be used in another punch for several weeks at least.

*Better no prayer than over-sacrifice,*
*A gift always looks for repayment,*
*Better no offering than too much slaughter,*
*So Thundr carved before human history* [16]

*I advise you secondly, that you should never swear an oath,*
*Unless you will keep it,*
*Grim wyrd goes with oathbreaking,*
*Wretched is such a varg* [17]

The life of warriorship revolves around the concept of Troth. This was the guiding principle which gave our ancestors a sense of direction and honour. Without Troth there could be no trust, co-operation, or society.

Troth is the bond of loyalty between the individual, the gods, kin, and the self. Being true to these principles is what makes us worthy. It is also the source of personal power. Through Troth we build our Wyrd. Every time we break Troth, we lose some footing on the slippery field of life's battle.

Because nobody is perfect, we must reaffirm our oaths at regular intervals. Rituals remind us of our direction and set the Wyrd in motion to assist us. It can be like recharging the batteries. Over time, we tend to become distracted by the humdrum of everyday life. We are constantly under pressure from our jobs, and from people in the media jostling to influence our opinions or our buying habits. It is easier than we

---

[16] Hávamál verse 145, my translation
[17] Sigrdrifumal verse 23, my translation

think to become swayed, little by little, until soon our true Will is forgotten.

There is little surviving in the literature about the details of ritual, but the important factors are discernible and do not change. Intent is the first of these, the will to bring about some kind of benefit for self and kin. It is important to be honest in this motive. Many are tempted to convince themselves (and others) that they are only motivated by some 'higher' purpose. Beware of this as it is a sure sign of self delusion and one path toward the Messiah complex.

The second factor is the link with ancestral power. By incorporating as many traditional features as we can reconstruct, we create a feeling of unity with the ancestors. This lays the foundation of the bridge which connects us to the power of the ancestral gods and spirits.

Third is repetition. Performing regular observances, whether daily or yearly, strengthens the link and the power of the working. It also retunes individuals with their Wills.

These rituals can be simple and are often more effective that way. Meals can be dedicated to fuelling the body to better do the Will's work. Even a new year's resolution can lift one out of a destructive rut. A well researched and well performed ritual has the potential to change lives in powerful and often unexpected ways.

It is useful at some point to choose a favourite deity and dedicate a period, even a lifetime, to working with that deity. If the choice is wise, this will open up a very close and personal relationship with part of the Northern pantheon and then on to a better understanding of the Northern spiritual culture as a whole.

The *Blót* or offering was common at seasonal festivals. The word *blot* comes from 'blood' as does the word 'bless', from the ancient practice of sprinkling the participants with the blood of the sacrificed[18]. The animal was usually an animal grown for meat, such as a pig or goat. There were also criminals sacrificed to Odin on occasions. These were usually hanged or strangled and stabbed with a spear at the same time.

While blóts of this form are rare, some feasts have been preceded in recent times by a ritual and humane killing of the night's dinner. One can sacrifice any object, as long as it is of some personal value or cost. It is pointless, even insulting to offer something that you would as easily throw away.

Equally important is to avoid offering too much. A moderate offering is a worthy gift of thanks, with the hope of a modest return if Wyrd allows. An excessive offering is tainted by the expectation of substantial reward. The gods are not so easily bought and do not appreciate someone trying to create obligation. A gift demands a gift. The wyrd returned may be what you asked for, but in a form not to your liking.

Setting up a small shrine or stall in or near your house is important. It provides a physical reminder and point of focus. A figurine on a special shelf along with symbols of that deity, perhaps also an offering bowl or drinking horn. Photographs of ancestors can be placed to each side.

An oath ring is also quite traditional attached to such an altar. It can be a finger, wrist, or arm ring made of iron, silver, or gold. The ring symbolises the binding of oaths to the wyrd. An oath made on such a ring would be witnessed by the god of the stall and bound to the wyrd of the warrior, even to the wyrd of other witnesses present. Such an oath always has serious repercussions indeed.

For those aspiring to the title of "Drighten", it should be remembered that it implies an oath of real leadership. Oaths of loyalty to a leader were not unconditional, nor was the title a mark of divine authority. The warrior's oath was a two-way contract. If the leader was consistently luckless or negligent, he

---

[18] cf the Kristjan practice of asperging - an obvious borrowing from Heathen practice

had effectively broken his contract and the warriors would leave him.

Another form of oath common amongst warriors is tattooing. Most in our society only see it as body art, but in all tribal cultures, including many of our ancestors, making permanent marks on the body signifies a serious rite of passage or major decision.

The very act of getting a tattoo or piercing will create significant change in the wyrd and the mind of the individual. It is common to see a youth's life go down hill after receiving a tattoo for frivolous reasons. A well timed and well designed tattoo, however, is a powerful boost to a warrior's wyrd and the ability to stay on course. Like any oath, serious thought should always go into the timing and design.

It is the nature of the wyrd that oaths will always have a wider field of influence than the oathmaker alone. For this reason many oaths should be made in the presence of the kindred. Feast nights are ideal for this purpose, and this tradition of toasting and oathmaking is called Symbel or Sumbl[19].

The feast itself is an important ritual of fellowship. Arguments can be set aside, friendships renewed, and new alliances made. Honour is on display, and the friendships made will be tested in due course. The fortune of each may rely on the troth of a friend. The survival of the group may depend on the honour of an individual.

At a point during the feast, when the clamour of greetings and the news from distant quarters has subsided, the horns are charged with the best mead saved for the Symbel. Each of the kin in turn makes three toasts. The first, to a hero or worthy ancestor. The second, to their own past achievements. And the third, an oath to a future deed or achievement.

The Symbel is a very powerful ritual of re-alignment of Kin, Will, and Wyrd. By toasting the ancestor/hero, we align ourselves with the admirable deeds of our people and their

---

[19] cf the modern English 'assembly'

past. We also re-affirm our kinship with our ancestors and invoke the power of their wyrd. This link with the ancestral folk is an essential part of the Northern tradition.

Recounting our own deeds to the assembled folk gives our own wyrd perspective. It encourages pride in our achievements. It also spurs us on to greater deeds. Just as important, it makes us aware of each other's deeds.

The oath of deeds to come makes us focus on what we really want to achieve. Once made, it binds us to success. Failure is dishonour and disempowerment. Wyrd, honour, and personal power become one with the third toast of the Symbel. As in any oath, the warriors' wyrd and hamingja, and that of their kin, are bound to the fulfilment of their oaths. With this in mind, we are compelled to consider carefully, and once made, our resolve to succeed will energise our actions and keep us heading in the right direction. From a word to a further word, on to a deed and further deeds.

*Sigrunes shalt thou know, if thou wilt have victory,*
*And carved on the hilt of your sword*
*Some on the pommel, and some on the guard,*
*And twice name Tyr* [20]

*Arguments and ale have been tragedy to many,*
*To some death, to some disaster,*
*Much is tragic to us* [21]

There is a long association in many cultures between self defence and magick. Our culture has its own tradition of magick in the martial arts. The sagas and the Havamal speak of victory runes and sigils of protection. These signs are most commonly runes, bindrunes, and helm of awe designs. They were usually scratched onto weapons and amulets.

The best known is the sig-rune of Tyr. Tiwaz, the upward pointing arrow, symbolises the rule of Law and the victory of True action. The Law of the one-handed god is action based on Troth. True action is decisive, without favour or prejudice and can be brutal. Carving this rune is an oath of success and a promise to win through impeccable action.

The bindrune, a combination of runes on a single stave, is a powerful method of concentrating intent. This is a working of tuning the warrior's will to the wyrd of the situation. This

---

[20] Sigrdrifumal verse 6, my translation
[21] Sigrdrifumal verse 30, my translation

requires skill and a deep knowledge of runelore. In every bindrune hidden runes work subtly. An ill wrought bindrune may achieve its purpose while reeking havoc along the way.

In a New-Age shop, I recently saw a commercial bindrune pendant sold as a protection for travellers. It was a cast pewter tile with the runes Raidho and Elhaz thrown together in a typically simplistic fashion. The result was a hidden (though rather obvious) Nauthiz emerging from the combination. Instead of protection while travelling, it would be more likely to provide protection from travelling. A perfect gift for someone you don't want going very far.

Creating effective bindrunes is a matter of experience and intuition backed up by a solid knowledge of runelore. Of all the types of sigils and magickal signs, bindrunes are perhaps the most difficult and dangerous. They invoke all the craft and cunning of the greatest of tricksters, Bølverkr himself.

Once skill has been achieved, and knowledge has become understanding, the warrior vitki can quickly formulate bindrunes for all occasions. Held briefly but clearly in the mind's eye, and projected onto the wyrd of the opponent or situation, the mark of one's will is invisibly and indelibly stamped onto the outcome.

Another type of sign used in this way is the Helm of Awe also known as the Helm of Terror. The original Helm first appears in the *Volsunga Saga* as part of a dragon's hoard which started off as weregild for the killing of an otter who happened to be somebody's relative.

As usual, it was Loki who committed the offence. He threw a fatal stone. The victim was the brother of Regin and Fafnir who went as an otter by day. As compensation to the powerful and wealthy father, the gods were required to fill the skin and cover the outside with gold. This was done, although Odin warned that the treasure would bring death.

The brother, Fafnir, killed the father in greed and hauled the gold off to a lair in the woods. Sitting alone on his hoard eventually turned Fafnir into a dragon.

Regin, having been deprived of his inheritance, told Sigurd (known to Wagnerians as Siegfried), who was one of our greatest legendary heroes. Regin reforged the broken sword which had belonged to Sigurd's father. The sword was the only one sharp and strong enough to pierce the dragon.

As Sigurd prepares to kill Fafnir and Regin hides in the woods at a safe distance, a stranger tells Sigurd how to avoid being killed by the dragon's blood. The stranger, obviously Odin, departs as mysteriously as he appeared.

As the dragon dies, he boasts of having borne the Helm of Terror and that no matter how many men had stood before him, he had thought himself stronger, and everyone was afraid of him. Sigurd replies that such a thing will not assure victory, because each warrior must eventually discover when in the company of many, that no one is the bravest of all.

The lesson we each must learn is that Odin has given the Helm of Terror to the dragon. Each of us must face and slay our dragon in order to take the Helm for ourselves. While the dragon uses the Helm to intimidate all who meet him, we must learn to use it with wisdom and discretion.

The dragon wears the Helm as a mask, to give the appearance of a terrible adversary. This is a false helm, it hides the dragon's own fear. Sigurd can wear the Helm to show that he has conquered fear. The Helm becomes a window into the warrior's true nature. This is the True Helm, a far more real and frightening taste of might.

With the Helm of Awe you will see your opponent's fear, and your opponent will glimpse your true being. The experience will empower you and demoralise your enemy. To master this knowledge, you must learn to know your opponent and see through an enemy's eyes. The more closely we know an enemy, the more certain our victory.

Get into your opponent's shoes in an instant. See from an alien perspective while remaining detached. Enter as if in a dance. Become your opponent and strike from within. Understand your enemy's motives, feel their every emotion, know their every movement, grasp their every fear. Let your enemies fight against their own wasted energy.

Become the perfect dance partner. Before you engage, show the terrible joy of your true face. Put on the True Helm of Terror, and lay waste the psychic battleground with the realisation that your enemy is self-defeated. This is one of the great secrets of victory. Beyond over-confidence, which is born of ego, there is a quiet knowledge and burning conviction, which stems from the warrior's intimacy with his or her 'victory wyrd'.

The most powerful victory working you can do before battle, is to invoke and bathe in the wyrd of all of your past successes and those of your ancestors, your kin, and your tradition. Wear this as the helm of your true nature, but also realise that your enemy must choose a path of self-destruction, and you must lead the way to its fulfilment.

As the Futhark is a system in our tradition which effects all areas of life and wyrd, you may use the runes to hone your inner warrior powers.

**Fehu:** To become aware of the circulation of energy between combatants. Face your sparring partner. Strike slowly exhaling, partner deflects slowly inhaling. Reverse roles. Alternating the strike and block phases, gradually increase the speed while staying in control. With practise, vary the strikes and blocks. Eventually, it will look like full on sparring, but will always be controlled.

On the wider scale, practice generosity with your kin.

**Uruz:** When sparring, practise advancing quickly while bending forward and weaving to the sides. Imagine thrusting horns, lead with the head. This is counter-intuitive at first. It is a natural reaction to pull the head away from trouble. Once comfortable with the head first attack, you will move more naturally and attack in a more committed and deadly fashion.

Practice quiet assertiveness rather than open aggression in the mundane world. Achieve your goals with patience and focus.

**Thurisaz:** You will need to feel for openings through which to strike. Without time for thought, you must learn to wait for these windows of opportunity to open, yet strike without hesitation when they do. You must also not be taken in by a feint. Begin as with the Fehu exercise, but this time feel for the moments when your partner loses contact or concentration. Do not think about it. When you can feel the openings, strike without thought; try it blindfolded.

Keep your senses sharp and ready for the unexpected. You will be rewarded by opportunities seized and disasters avoided.

**Ansuz:** You will need to use intelligence to outsmart your opponents before you come to blows. Often, you can win without a fight. Practice debating with intellectual equals. Pit your wits against each other in games of knowledge or strategy. Know as much as possible about your potential enemies. Invoke the trickiness of Odin.

Use this every day, in every situation, but be careful not to become too arrogant.

**Raidho:** Movement must be natural yet controlled by will. Practice judging distances and moving quickly into the best position. Adapt your moves to dance and let yourself flow with the rhythm. Learn to play a drum and work on increasingly complex beats and changes.

Work on being aware of your situation within the structure of the various laws.

**Kenaz:** This involves the understanding of the malleable nature of any situation. Visualise and project your willed outcome onto the event. Mentally heat or cool the situation to your benefit. In a more free form sparring, make note of the structure of the combat. You will notice every bout assumes a form and rhythm. When this becomes apparent, shift suddenly into a different stance and timing. Destroy the form with sudden chaos, and before the opponent can adjust, attack with new rhythm, direction, and techniques.

At all times be aware of alternative methods to get things done. Often it will clear a stalemate if you can cause shift in the ground-rules and use the ensuing chaos to dash for the finish line.

**Gebo:** A gift demands a gift. As we have seen, not in the sense of a tally sheet, but in the way every action creates an imbalance which will bring about a reaction of some kind. One of the most difficult things to achieve in combat is a state of harmony and balance within the maelstrom. It can only be achieved by practice and honesty. Detachment is essential. Stay loose and keep your position optimal in relation to your opponent's. Cultivate a feeling of working in co-operation with your opponent, even when fighting to the death. Each combat is a gift of valuable lessons to both parties.

Practise keeping your word, hospitality, and repaying debts before having to be reminded.

**Wunjo:** This is the support of your kin. In combat, it is the ability to fight as a team. Sometimes it is necessary to defend yourself and the group you are in. If you are in a small group facing multiple attackers, you must be able to defend yourselves and each other without getting in each other's way. Practise group sparring and team games. Experience the joy and satisfaction of winning as a team.

Hold regular social events, particularly feasts and symbels. Encourage health, happiness, and fellowship amongst your kin.

**Hagalaz:** While the first eight runes were utilised, practised, and experienced in a fairly physical way, the second eight involve a more internal, mental approach. They involve the most difficult of the warrior's ordeals, the conquest of mind. Hagalaz is the seed of your will and wyrd in Midgard. It is also a rune of crisis. It can be visualised as a white hailstone or point of light at the solar plexus. Make this your centre of gravity, and centre of action in battle. Move from this untouchable point, and you will find that you will be able to walk through an attack. This is also a cure for head shyness, the problem of stiffness caused by trying to hold the head away from the action (see also Uruz).

When faced with any crisis, open yourself to all possibilities. Elements of the disaster will become the seed of a better start.

**Nauthiz:** A constant companion of the warrior. We must feel a real need to follow this path. There will be many obstacles, both external and internal, which could persuade us to seek a more comfortable existence. This need will, and must, be spontaneous at first. As things become more difficult, need must be cultivated consciously. Think about defending someone important to you. Imagine how you would feel if your lack of training allowed them to be killed or raped. Generate an almost desperate need to improve.

Practise discipline, set yourself both tasks and boundaries. Go without something for a set period. You will learn to overcome any limitation.

**Isa:** Ice is the element of contraction, the line between one move and the next. Become aware of the pauses between moves. These may be almost too short to perceive at first, but once perceived, they offer both rest and power. Explode from the stillness of Ice.

Practise the meditation technique already discussed. Learn the power of silence.

**Jera:** We must all learn to anticipate the consequences of our actions. More than this, we must learn to act to optimise our outcomes. Never rush into battle unprepared. Sometimes you will be caught by surprise, but a little forethought before approaching a situation will mean the difference between life and death. Acquire alliances, skills, and suitable weaponry.

Consider every act to be an investment to be harvested later.

**Eihwaz:** To the warrior, this rune is present in the realisation of the fine line between life and death. It is the same line as that between sanity and madness. The mystery of yew in this context is the understanding, a knowing at a deep level, that we can walk this line and survive as long as we remember that every step is our own decision. We are free to choose the options within our wyrd. Every moment is a choice point.

When Isa has cleared the mind of its constant chatter, the working of Eihwaz will become clear. Scry the blade's edge.

**Perthro:** Orlog, the primal layer, the ultimate reality of anything. Working with wyrd gives us a glimpse at orlog. Taking responsibility for our own wyrd, and actively participating in its unfolding, instead of being trapped in it, will allow us to work with orlog itself, instead of the shadow play we normally call reality.

Start realising that in life you can effect the roll of the dice. Take hold of the lot cup and play to win.

**Elhaz:** Known as a rune of protection, this is the link between our divine connections and our self defence. The sword alone is of little effect until it is wielded with divine inspiration. Before training, stand in the Elhaz stadha and call on the gods and ancestors to inspire your combat.

Practise being true to your way at all times. This is the protection of the sword.

**Sowilo:** The protection of the shield. The sun symbolises the illumination of the world by consciousness. Its effectiveness is measured by success in Midgard. This success depends on decisions based on sound thinking and good advice. Seek those who can advise well. Learn to accept the help of others, but be self-reliant.

Discuss relevant issues with intelligent friends. Give and take good advice. Practise solving logical puzzles.

**Tiwaz:** The third eight runes refer to the relationship of the warrior to the world and its inhabitants and lead to the knowledge of the spiritual self. Hold troth within your mind. Understand the law as it relates to you. Learn the rules of nature, society, and the legal system. Balance these laws with your intuition. Practise moving fluidly within the lines of law toward a clear victory.

Observe how rules and events interact. Use this knowledge to succeed.

**Berkano:** The protection of concealment. Learn when to talk, to whom, and how much. The wartime saying 'loose lips sink ships'. Many of your plans will never reach fruition if they become public knowledge. An opponent will use any information about you to thwart you. Also keep what you know about your opponent secret until you need to use it. A seed planted needs time to germinate undisturbed.

Try always to keep some aces up your sleeve.

**Ehwaz:** At most times in life there will be someone in whom you must place trust and loyalty. This may be a best friend, a mentor, or spouse. Our ancestors had a tradition of blood brotherhood in which they lifted a turf and mixed their blood in the earth beneath it. Such a bond is of the greatest consequence.

Work closely with another, and practice trust, but do not become dependent.

**Mannaz:** Humanity. Knowing the basic nature of yourself and your foe. It is essential to be able to predict another's state of mind. This rune is particularly important in matters of revenge, which will be covered in a later chapter.

Practise seeing from the perspective of others.

**Laguz:** Primeval waters of life. From the depths of Urdh's well the unmanifest unknown is drawn up into manifestation. This connects us all at a much more primal level than Mannaz. It is the Laguz energies that a 'vampire' (the real human kind) will try to drain from you. They manifest most strongly as emotional and sexual energies within a group dynamic.

Become aware of the manipulation of emotional and sexual energies at parties.

**Ingwaz:** The hero's retreat. The warrior must periodically withdraw from society to work on inner growth. Without these breaks, you will slowly lose your independence of will. No matter how strong we are, our integrity will gradually be eroded by the manipulations of others, the media, and other social pressures. Regular retreats for meditation and training will keep you energised and focused.

Spend a few minutes a day meditating. Take a week off at least once a year to be alone and silent.

**Dagaz:** This, for the Odinic warrior, is the essence of conscious life. We seek the extremes and can be found in unexpected company. The ability to mix in any scene, yet never become immersed in the social games of that scene. This gives us the advantage of being able to participate in any social situation while remaining detached. To our friends, we seem paradoxical. To strangers, we do not stand out, unless we choose to.

Make a point of moving in completely different circles, fit in, but don't get sucked in.

**Othala:** The ultimate aim is the gaining of our ancestral heritage. Within the enclosure of our holy stead lies the key to our rightful inheritance. This stead is our manifestation in Midgard, built on the foundations laid by the ancestors. Ultimately, we recognise no authority save that within ourselves. But it takes much work, discipline, and wisdom to learn to distinguish this treasure from the fools gold and glitter pumped into our thoughts by the small minds of townsfolk and the all-permeating persuasions of corporate greed.

Honour the ancestors, particularly those who were warriors and risked all to ensure our freedom and manifestation in Midgard. Observe the Einherjar days, November 11, also April 25 ANZAC day in Australia & New Zealand, various Veterans days in the countries you are in.

*A cowardly man thinks he will live forever*
*If he can avoid fighting*
*But old age will give him no mercy*
*Though he be spared by spears* [22]

Magickal weapons are a very ancient tradition in the North. Swords in particular appear with names and often personalities. A weapon inherited from a famous forebear is perhaps the most powerful kind. A sword received from a king was also considered special.

A major difference between the Asatruar and the ceremonial magicians is revealed in the attitude toward magickal weapons. The ceremonialist insists on 'ritual purity' involving the careful separation of these weapons from anything 'mundane'. It is considered a severe contamination to use a magickal tool or weapon for any purpose outside of the prescribed ritual. A sword which had ever been stained with blood would be useful only to a 'black magician'.

To the Heathen, however, there exists no such artificial separation between magickal and mundane. The Wyrd of the weapon is enhanced by any action which carries the intent of the magician's Will. All acts are magickal in that every thought, word, and deed has an impact on the individual's Wyrd.

The magickal power of our weapons lies in their Wyrd. The more we train with them, look after them, and defeat our

---

[22] Hávamál verse 16, my translation

enemies with them (in ritual or self defence), the greater their power in our hands. When we use them in ritual, they will be all the more effective and worthy in that function. Always respect weaponry, both your own and other's.

If we separate our magick and religion from our everyday lives, we risk relegating our tradition to a roleplay. Our personal and group worth will only be judged by our efforts in Midgard. It is easy to fall into the delusions of grandeur, dressed in fine tunics at a seasonal feast. Ask yourself what you really want to achieve in your life and how far you have gone toward achieving it.

True Will motivates us with an urge for creativity. False desires are motivated by fear. If we analyse the messages coming to us from society, compelling us through advertising or moralising, they are all based on fear. We are urged to conform or risk missing out on something, suffering social disapproval, or some other unpleasantness. Rarely are we tempted by a genuine need, or warned of a genuine danger.

The intersection of Wyrd, Will, Weapons, and the binding oath, was represented on some swords by a ring attached to the hilt. Although mainly seen on Kentish swords in the actual ring form, swords elsewhere often had a representation of a ring on the hilt decoration indicating that the ring was not merely for attaching a thong.

Adding to the magical power of a weapon is the intent of the owner. The more we work with such weapons, the more power they gain, and the more confidence we gain. This mutual strengthening will aid the warrior in all situations, even when the weapon is not immediately available. In grave need, the wyrd of the weapon can be called upon to tip the balance, though the weapon itself is not at hand.

The weapon itself need not be a traditional one. If called on to defend self and folk, it is unlikely that a warrior would choose anything but the most effective weapon available. There are some in Heathen and Pagan circles who seem suspicious of technology, but it must be remembered that our ancestors have always been quite keen on developing and utilising the best technology available to them.

If under physical attack, a fire-arm is often most effective. If our traditions are attacked by ignorance, books are most appropriate. If we face becoming an invisible and irrelevant minority, our best tool is the Internet. It will take clever use of all of our resources to resist the creeping homogenisation of our culture. The Internet may be full of New Age waffle, but all the more reason for us to stand out as a more powerful and authentic alternative. No other medium has given us a better platform upon which to be visible to all who seek to know the truth about our way.

An effective warrior keeps an open mind with regard to the usefulness of potential tools and weapons. While some may may be seduced into the partial worlds, and perhaps fantasy worlds, which evolve in any medium, whether TV world, web world, book world, or academia, we can not afford to dismiss the substantial effects these worlds have on the "Real World" of Midgard. The warrior looks into each of these worlds and uses each with full consciousness, recognising each as a partial and imperfect view, and assessing each for its potential real uses.

The fastest path to extinction is the opposite form of escapism, shunning the tools of the modern world, either out of a sense of puritanism, or misplaced traditionalism, or fear of learning something new. Do not forget that our ancestors were innovators and technologists who made impressive advances in shipbuilding and metalurgy. We can not live in the past, but must be ready for the future. One thing we can learn from the past is that those who fail to adapt do not survive.

Now getting back to physical defence. The key to survival is the mastery of fear. Most of us try to avoid situations which may result in violence. An attacker will rely on this to induce a state of anxiety in their victim. The attack will usually consist initially of verbal threat reinforced with superficial pain. For most victims, the effect will be instant demoralisation, fear, and a feeling that it is just not fair. Such a reaction robs the victim of the will to mount a defence.

The muggers continue to do it, because they get away with it, because they rarely come across any real resistance. Our ancestors would be sickened by this fact. By training ourselves out of the victim mentality, we can do something to help ourselves and our kin. By mastering fear, we can instantly reverse the situation. The only response acceptable in this situation is a 100% commitment to a decisive, devastating, and utterly merciless victory. Any hesitation is defeat.

Faced with such danger, the attackers will become demoralised and fall easy prey to the wrath of Odin, Tyr, and Thor.

Legalists will ask at this point, "what about the concept of minimum force?". While I will discuss the legal implications in a later chapter, it is important to this discussion to know that the legal definition of self defence is the use of the minimum amount of force necessary to avoid serious injury or death to yourself or a person you may be defending.

Obviously, if you kill someone for spitting on you, you will go to jail. You must use your judgement about the proportionality of your response. Even so, this principle involves a great degree of subjectivity on the part of a jury.

One thing I learned, both in the Army and in the martial arts, is that while minimum force is taught in theory, it is not always wise or possible to apply it. In practice, the application of the minimum force rule will only put you in unnecessary danger. If there is a real threat to your bodily integrity, only maximum force will ensure your survival. Anything less than a 100% effort will leave you open to failure and death.

If you leave an attacker functioning, he will either kill you or sue you. If deadly force is threatened, if you are in real danger, it is best to kill your attacker outright as swiftly as possible. If you hesitate after you deal the first blow, it could be argued in court that your second blow constituted a second attack, and that the opponent was no longer capable of doing harm. This will negate your self defence argument in court. On the other hand, if you hesitate after the first blow, your attacker could recover enough to kill you.

In such a battle, emotion must be set aside. Strike with techniques honed to scalpel sharpness, with surgical accuracy and with the determination of an endurance athlete. The speed, skill, and knowledge are essential, but they will fail if seized by fear. Once your counter attack is in progress, it must not relent until total victory is certain. Become your own magickal weapon.

*Keep your eyes open when entering,*
*always wary, always watchful,*
*You never know if an enemy,*
*May sit in hiding within the hall* [23]

*I know a third, if I am in great need of fettering foes,*
*Blades I blunten, of my enemies,*
*No longer will their weapons bite* [24]

Many of the sagas and poems of our traditions speak of the long hours spent in the mead hall playing games of skill and chance. Such games were more than mere amusement.

Games of this kind are useful both for honing skills and for testing a warrior's wyrd. As we have seen, personal power and wyrd are closely intertwined. Indeed any situation can be thought of as a game, only the stakes differ. Thus a warrior must learn the rules and the risks.

In any game there are times when the rules can be bent. The bending of rules is governed by higher level rules, the social or legal ones. The bending of higher level rules is governed by the warrior's perception of wyrd and honour. As each situation is unique, no set of rules can hope to cover every possible eventuality.

---

[23] Hávamál verse 1, my translation
[24] Hávamál verse 148, my translation

At the highest level there is the law of nature, Ørlog, the primal layer. This law, by definition, cannot be broken, no matter what we do. The gods themselves are subject to their wyrd which is a manifestation of their interaction with Ørlog. Sometimes it will be necessary to break lower level rules in order to appease higher levels of obligation or constraint. Skill resides in the dance through the multi-level maze of rules which govern our lives.

To learn this skill, we must become aware that even a simple game of dice is governed by a hierarchy of five levels of constraint. First, the rules of the game. Second, the rules of social propriety. Third, the legal system of the land. Fourth, the wyrd resulting from our previous actions. And fifth, Ørlog, which manifests wyrd, friction, gravity, and any other inescapable law of the universe. Each level up the hierarchy introduces greater constraint and greater possible risk.

The most important factor in the successful navigation of this maze is timing.

One thing to remember about most games is that they are simplified representations of aspects of combat. Unfortunately, most people seem to view all situations of conflict from a highly simplified perspective. One thing the Sagas do make clear is that most conflicts are highly complex, and a recurring theme is the personal turmoil of being forced to choose sides when loyalties are owed to both sides.

Whenever an international conflict arises there are a multitude of people eager to express their support for one side or the other without even a basic understanding of the complexities of the situation. It is the most common practice to choose one side because of personal prejudice or "political correctness", and demonise the other. This kind of thinking allows dictators to prosper.

There are few conflicts in which one side has a clear claim of moral superiority, but in these cases we owe support to those groups whose distinct identity is threatened by the faceless monocultural machine of oppression, centralised authority, corporate greed, and the churches. Anthropologists call this process 'acculturation', the destruction of a people's culture.

There are many ways to offer support to such a people. We may one day be grateful for their support in return. This does not mean we should sacrifice our own warriors in their cause, we need to preserve them for our own defence.

You can make modest donations of money. Get a bumper sticker, or write a letter, or find some other way to bring the situation to the attention of the public. I suggest you choose one and learn the facts. I have chosen the Tibetans who have been decimated and acculturated in their own country. You may choose the tribes of the Amazon, or Borneo whose cultures are destroyed by missionaries and the greed of outsiders, or the marginalised tribes of Burma. If we tolerate the destruction of other cultures, it will only be a matter of time before ours too falls before the steamroller of homogenisation.

But in backing causes beware. As I have said, most conflicts are not so easily read, most involve minorities within minorities, and factions within each, all with differing allegiances and motives. Identifying the victims depends upon your perspective. It is a mistake to take sides in such a conflict thinking that one side has a moral superiority.

Many conflicts today involve this type of scenario: an enclave of tribe A who feel victimised by their more numerous neighbours, tribe B who own the surrounding region and who in turn feel threatened by a larger neighbouring region dominated by tribe A. The enclave A may have existed for centuries, it is their home, why should they move to region A, or be assimilated by tribe B and lose their ethnic heritage? Tribe B, however, wants to fully own its ancestral region and feels the enclave A is an incursion of region A into its lands. Why should tribe B tolerate its perceived enemies on its soil?

How large should a population be to deserve self determination? How long should it be resident to own its land?

Clearly, neither side can claim a superior position on moral grounds. Both sides will have been guilty of offences against the other. In reality, the situation is likely to be much more complicated, with a history which shows both sides at fault. These types of conflict are often characterised by atrocities and terrorism. For an outsider to express support for either side in such a conflict is neither intelligent nor honourable.

Often, your combat these days will be in the form of the written word. This is truly the domain of Odin. Wit and subtlety are the weapons needed. In this arena, victory is assured to those who truly grasp Odin's gift. There are three main types of word-battle in which we are likely to become involved.

Firstly, the traditional poetry war. This usually occurs in a public forum, but is hidden from those not in the know by the use of kennings and obscure imagery. To outsiders, the poetry will mean little, or will apply to fairly general situations. To those in the know, it may be extremely direct and insulting. There is a great deal of skill involved in crafting words to hit hard at a select audience while offering few clues to others.

Secondly, open public discourse. Often we find ourselves defending our ideas or traditions from the less informed. A decisive victory involves having superior information to offer and making the opponent look small without making your reply look petty, too arrogant, or an over-reaction. If you have specific information about your opponents, you can use it subtly to draw an over-reaction from them. The apparently unwarranted, and usually personal, attack on you will cost them credibility. This arena is our most important in determining our reputation in the wider community.

Thirdly, private correspondence. Here there are no holds barred, as long as you do not leave yourself open to your words being later used against you. It is often wise to let your opponents think you are on the back foot, drawing them out. They will often become over-confident and reveal too much. Just as they begin to gloat, move in for the kill.

The decisive stroke in any of these conflicts should leave no room for any reasonable reply. Use wit and subtlety to convey the impression that you know their minds and are totally unaffected by their attack. As in physical combat, the final reply should be cold, surgical, and devastating, leaving the attacker unable to make a further move without looking desperate or foolish.

Do not be drawn into making a hasty reply in anger. Like physical combat, your attacker will be trying to humiliate and anger you. There is plenty of time to consider your reply. Look carefully at the previous messages and you will begin to get a picture of the person's mind, their weaknesses, what their real motivations might be, details about their present situation. If they are attacking anonymously, you may be able to work out who they are, or at least the group or tradition they come from. Often you will gain an intuitive knowledge of details about their gender, nationality, political leaning, etc.

Remember that many of the techniques in this book, even if not physically harmful, are for use with those whose enmity is serious. Do not use them lightly. Keep in mind the Nine Noble Virtues, of which if you are reading this book, you should already be very familiar. If not, you should read up on basic Asatru in the many popular works available. Also remember another great virtue, magnanimity, which is the key to immense personal power.

*I know a fourth, if enemies bind my arms and legs,*
*I have spells to free me, fly the fetters from my feet,*
*And the bonds from my hands* [25]

When I first suggested this book, I asked a few people what they would like to see in it. I have tried to cover as many of these angles as possible. One suggestion was a description of historical fighting techniques. For a number of reasons I have not chosen to pursue this.

Firstly, techniques differed between places and times, and also between individuals. Secondly, there is not enough detail in the evidence to draw any useful conclusions about hand-to-hand techniques. Thirdly, having taught hand-to-hand techniques in a martial art school, I know how hard it is to convey a useful understanding of the subtleties of any particular technique even when one is intimately familiar with it.

I have seen some examples of styles based on runic postures. We can say nothing about the age or authenticity of these except that no evidence exists that such techniques existed before recent times. To be fair, their adherents are genuine and derive a great deal from their practice. My personal feeling is that these forms seem a little too rigid from an Odinic perspective and appear more suited to a Tyric path. The tricky, fluid, shape-shifting styles seem to me to express more of the Odinic character. As for pre-Kristjan combat forms, the evidence is just too sparse and open to interpretation, although

---

[25] Hávamál verse 149, my translation

one Northern tradition combat system which does look very effective and well researched is STAV (details in the reference section at the end of the book).

There has, however, been some good research into battle tactics. The Germanic tribes, and particularly the Vikings, were known for their ability to trick the enemy into making tactical mistakes. A typical manoeuvre would be for the battle line to break in the middle and start to run as if in route. The enemy line would chase them into the gap only to have the running warriors suddenly turn and form a shield wall. The disorganised chasing troops would find themselves closed in on all sides with deadly shield walls.

The trick is to take advantage of your enemy's greed for victory, money, or revenge. It is often easy to tempt an opponent into sacrificing the battle for the sake of an apparent short term gain.

Another technique mentioned in the Sagas is the Battle Fetter. Some warriors were credited with the ability to cause an opponent to freeze. This effect is possible to replicate with practice and a good practical knowledge of psychology and physiology. These techniques work by causing disorientation. This can be achieved in a number of ways, usually involving a combination of physical and psychological manipulation.

Any sudden marked change in one's immediate environment will cause a moment of distraction or confusion as new data is processed. In some combinations, these changes flood the senses with too much new data and the individual will stall or become unco-ordinated for a moment. This state may last for a fraction of a second to several seconds, depending on the skill of the fetter. Even a brief gap in your enemy's attack will be enough for a decisive strike to get through.

In any system of martial art, you will start with a list of main techniques to which you will gradually add further techniques and variations. No matter how many techniques you collect, it will not really become an art until the principles and philosophy of the style are understood at an intuitive level. Suddenly, you will find that the list of isolated forms becomes a whole greater than the sum of its parts, like cells forming the body of an organism, each playing a part in a living individual entity.

The only way to achieve the integration of a style is through constant practise and regular contact with a teacher who has achieved this integration. This is a long term project and should ideally be started at an early age, but for many older students maturity and judgement more than compensate for physical prowess.

Once learned, your combat style will evolve to make the most of your changing body, mind, and environment. Speed and resilience will generally peak at about 25 years of age, allowing a very energetic expression of the style. Physical strength and toughness tend to peak at around 35, allowing a more deliberate, crushing, and inexorable kind of battle. Strategic thinking and cunning will result from mature experience, usually peaking at 45, but when combined with good fitness and exercise, can continue to improve almost indefinitely.

It is a common mistake for age groups to underestimate each other. An awareness of the age of your opponent will allow you to estimate some of their likely strengths and weaknesses. Keep in mind, however, that few people conform completely to categories. Use all of the information you can acquire, in the time available, to build a picture of an enemy before committing yourself to action. Conversely, give away as little information about yourself as possible.

By focusing on the principles rather than the techniques, you will become less transparent to an attacker. There are also times when a favourite technique will not work. If the principles have become intuitive, you will be able to alter your movement to take advantage of any change in the dynamics of the situation. An attacker will not be able to manoeuvre you into a difficult position.

As a part of warriorship, the combat principles you learn can be applied to all areas of life. Discipline, flexibility, strategic thinking, and the ability to stay calm and see the larger perspective. These along with physical fitness, allow the warrior to succeed in any endeavour. This is what makes a true warrior. Skill in battle is of little use if you do not have a life worth fighting for.

As I keep saying, the measure of your attainment can only be seen by its reflection in Midgard. It is important to practice applying your skills to various arts and sciences, and particularly to your job. The principles of your martial art will thus become more fully incorporated into your life and will in turn become more effective in your combat style.

*Think not that hatred and feuds are lulled to sleep*
*Any more than sorrow*
*Wits and weapons both should an atheling acquire*
*He who shall be foremost* [26]

No discussion of Northern warriorship would be complete without mention of the berserkers. Many of the sagas describe a particular sort of warrior who was characterised by the ability to enter an altered state of mind.

The nature of the art of Berserkergang was little understood by the average Viking, much less by the modern academic. Many Sagas make little distinction between foul tempered bullies and those devotees of Odin who became divinely inspired, wading into the sea of blades, seemingly invincible.

In the Sagas, berserkers were said to have fought without body armour and yet survive unscathed. Sometimes they even went without the psychological advantage of a layer of clothing between their skin and the enemy's sword.

In our tradition, the symbolism of removing the armour is of great importance, but before it is safe to do so, one must be adept at doing battle fully armoured. Whether on the battlefield or in the marketplace we all wear some sort of armour against 'the slings and arrows of outrageous fortune', or more to the point, the barbs of our fellow humans. In order to operate efficiently we must know our strengths and

---

[26] Sigrdrifumal verse 36, my translation. Atheling = noble person

weaknesses and become aware of the style and construction of our armour.

As our movements become increasingly efficient, we find that we can afford to shed some of our armour. We then find that our movements become even more efficient with the resulting freedom. Eventually we find ourselves totally open to the world. No longer encumbered with layers of protection we are free to be our true selves. Every act becomes a spontaneous and joyous act of pure will. We become a vortex of pure will force.

Paradoxically, while a novice stripped of armour would be instantly slain, an adept becomes impervious to steel. The berserk ceases to be a target by becoming as if devoid of gross substance. The *Ynglinga Saga* describes the Berserks when inspired by Odin, "They cut down the enemy, while neither fire nor iron could make an impression on them." That which offers no resistance cannot be cut. That which is flexible cannot be broken.

Anyone who has been in combat situations will realise that uncontrolled anger is rarely a friend in battle. Such emotion may well stimulate enthusiasm and fearlessness, but at the cost of judgement and precision; there is a Samurai saying, "The angry man will defeat himself in battle as well as in life"[27]. The true berserk rage is certainly not blind anger. An angry warrior may be frightening and deadly but is unlikely to come out of a battle alive, let alone unscathed.

There is in certain circles, the belief that drugs were used to induce the rage, in particular *Amanita Muscaria* [28]. While the use of drugs in occult training is almost universal, and the training of berserks most probably included them, there is no evidence that they were ever taken to induce the rage. Gordon Wasson, who studied in great depth the historical use of *Amanita Muscaria*, presents in detail the recent origin of this myth, and the reasons for dismissing it, in his epic work *Soma, The Divine Mushroom*. Our point of view is that, as with anger,

---

[27] Zen in the Martial Arts, J Hyams
[28] Fly Agaric mushroom

drugs would tend to diminish the precision of a warrior's actions.

The secret of the berserk's invulnerability is the ability to let the True Will flow unimpeded. This requires the warrior to be totally calm and centred while at the same time unleashing the destructive forces of the Will. This is a form of meditation infinitely more difficult than being calm and centred in a quiet room (something most people find almost impossible anyway). The slightest distracting thought can be fatal. By not letting thoughts interfere with the flow of Will, the berserk is always in the right place at the right time. Action flows, there is no rigidity or predictability, there is nowhere a blade can strike.

The berserk acts without hesitation and is always in harmony with any situation. Harmony in this case means being true to the self and interacting with the situation in a way which is honest with the self. This can only be done when there is no barrier between the self and the situation. One becomes a fluid part of the situation without losing one's individuality, an indispensable yet autonomous part of the whole, every movement being a vital adjustment of one's position in the universe.

The true nature of the berserk state cannot be imagined or surmised, it can only be experienced. As in any work of magick or combat, the only measure of success is its manifestation in Midgard. Bear skins and wolf skins are powerful symbols in our tradition, but they can not create berserkers, any more than mind altering substances can.

We must learn to recognise and face real danger with a clear mind, and allow our training and instincts to work for our will. The problem we face in our training is finding real danger without incurring foolish risks. Perhaps the best solution is to find those fears which most motivate, and by fully experiencing them, conquer them. This is a very personal quest, but there are also the common ones.

We are all endowed with a natural fear of pain. It is important in training to experience enough pain to overcome this fear without risking serious injury. Full contact sparring, with carefully planned rules, will enable us to ignore pain for long enough to get the job done. Unfortunately, nothing can fully prepare us for a real situation, so when it happens, view it as a rare and valuable opportunity to hone skills.

It will pay to be exposed regularly to unfamiliar, confusing, or frightening environments. Pain, fear, and confusion need not incapacitate us. By training with these in a controlled environment, we will be more able to accept and work with extreme situations when necessary. But coping is not enough, we must also be calm enough to see and understand the flow of events, clear enough to gauge the dangers, and confident enough to take control.

When faced with a sudden and extreme change in our environment, such as a natural disaster or a physical attack, the initial enemy is confusion. Master the art of being calm in the maelstrom, and confusion becomes your ally. While the average person can be seen wandering in a daze, those with Odinn's gift will appear quite at home.

*He is happy, who gains for himself
reputation and popularity
Uncomfortable the position of the man
who must depend on the mind of another* [29]

*Reticent and thoughtful should be the noble's heir
and courageous in battle
Glad and cheerful should a man be
Until he meets his end* [30]

Once trained in the mental, spiritual, and physical disciplines of the Heathen Warrior, we acquire responsibilities. These will dictate the use of our deadly powers.

If attacked, it is the duty of the warrior to defend self and kinfolk. Unfortunately, physical injury is only half the danger you face if you ever need to defend yourself with force. Once trained, your encounter will probably be over in seconds. This is when your real defence effort begins.

As you stand over your vanquished foe, you will need to think carefully about making a statement to the Police. Like a job interview, first impressions can determine the way you will be perceived and treated in subsequent interviews.

Laws vary from state to state and between countries, but most legal systems will base their view of your action on the concept of 'reasonable force'. This principle states that you may legally

---

[29] Hávamál verse 8, my translation
[30] Hávamál verse 15, my translation

defend yourself against an attack providing you did nothing to provoke it, you could not find an alternative way out, and you took measures only sufficient to neutralise the threat, no more.

In court, if your opponent's injuries are serious, you will need to convince a jury that you had a reasonable and real belief that you were in immediate danger of serious bodily harm or death.

If you can convince the Police that you had no choice, you may avoid being charged with assault. If charged, Police testimony will be a vital factor in court. If you are lucky you will be acquitted without too much legal expense. Your troubles however, do not end here. It is possible that your attacker may sue for damages, particularly if there is any doubt about the exact details of the incident.

It is vital for the Warrior to understand the Law fully, both in general principles and local specifics as it applies to situations in which we may find ourselves. Laws relating to the possession and use of weapons tend to vary quite a bit between jurisdictions. Self defence, however, is a fairly consistent principle. The dilemma faced by the modern warrior is that you may face a situation in which you have to technically break the law in order to survive the fight, and then have to be creative with the truth in order to survive the courts.

Local laws are quite specific about the types of weapon which are completely banned, those which are illegal to carry in a public place, and those which are illegal to carry concealed. Some jurisdictions get around the need to define what constitutes a weapon by allowing the courts to decide that an item (be it screwdriver, spray-can, or anything else) was being carried without 'lawful purpose' (eg. NSW Crimes Act). Under this law you may be searched on suspicion and be fined for being in possession of any item for which you have no reasonable explanation. This is a good thing when used on gangs, or vandals with paint cans, but it has caught otherwise innocent folk who just want a fighting chance in case of an attack, particularly women with spray-cans.

If you decide to carry a weapon, be sure to research the local laws thoroughly. Also be aware how the use of weapons effect your legal claim of self-defence. If the court decides that you had a significant advantage over your opponent, you may not be able to use self-defence as an effective argument against prosecution for assault or murder.

Another theme which was a popular subject of our ancestor's tales was revenge. Revenge has been given a bad name by the petty and spiteful form it most often assumes. This has been true since ancient times. But there was a time when a truly poetic vengeance was admired as a work of art.

I have just drawn a rune from my divination bag. Wyrd has given me Mannaz as a focus for this discussion. Not surprisingly, Odin's oracle is both ironic and appropriate, evoking a familiar grim smile. Intelligence, an awareness of our human nature, even empathy with the victim are essential.

Although the story of Wayland survived only as a poem in the Eddas, it was well known to the Germanic peoples. This is indicated in an earlier (pre-Edda) Anglo-Saxon poem, *Deor's Lament*, which refers to characters in the Wayland story and assumes the listener has substantial knowledge of the tale[31].

Wayland was admired not only for his skill in metals, but equally for the skill and intelligence of his masterpiece of revenge. He exemplifies the principle of Mannaz. Resisting the temptation to satisfy base emotion by taking hasty action, Wayland uses his powers of empathy to understand the emotional attachments of the Niara king and queen. Yet he never allows himself to fall into the mistake of attachment or sympathy with them.

For most people the only choice is between a hasty retaliation, usually with unfortunate repercussions (Thor), or to repress the urge and suffer the resulting stress along with the possibility of further advantage being taken (Kristjan). The wise divest themselves of their troubles with the quiet oath

---

[31] See The Lay of Volund, *The Poetic Edda*, transl L Hollander. Also *The Earliest English Poems*, Penguin Classics

"when the time is right..." (Odin & Wayland). Time can be our ally, while both haste and hesitation are deadly enemies. Feel when to strike with devastating speed , and when to wait for plague and old age to sweep your foes into oblivion. Wyrd will instruct you, and wyrd will fulfill the doom you set in motion.

Mannaz imbues the avenger with intelligence and an understanding of human wyrd. With awareness of the subtle flow of forces between self and victim, the window of opportunity becomes clear. Nothing is wasted. The avenger need not sacrifice anything of value in the act. It would be senseless to give up life or liberty for a vendetta.

The purpose of revenge is to teach a hard lesson, to prevent further offence, and to redress the balance of wyrd. As Wayland illustrates, it is better not to focus on the enemy, but to target the enemy's attachments. It is better not to act with aggression, but to entice the victim into a voluntary sacrifice. Use these attachments to bait a trap which will rob the victim of those very attachments.

Most important in this process is your own state of mind. Do not act in anger. Do not think of yourself as the victim. Always see the offender as the victim. Do not brood over the offence or the wer-geld (*Vergeltung*). Cultivate a detached amusement at your victim's impending disaster, yet view the lesson as a compassionate gift. Such mental discipline and detachment is only possible in the individuated consciousness embodied in Mannaz.

Remember the way of Odin, don't get mad, get even.

*Then will it be proven, what you learned from the runes,*
*Of holy making, by mighty powers,*
*And carved by the Great Sage,*
*Then will one best keep silent* [32]

The problem with modern society is that it makes people dependent and irresponsible. Despite being more educated than ever, people remain in a childlike state of dependence. Laws are increasingly focused on keeping the citizen from harming himself.

In traditional warrior societies, people were initiated into adulthood. Children were barred from playing with dangerous things, but a trained and initiated adult was expected to be armed and ready to defend the tribe at all times. This training and initiation is not a common process any more. Modern democracy treats all as equals. One need only pass a certain age to qualify as adult. The result is that either we end up with a disarmed and defenceless population as in Australia, or weapons legally owned by even the most unworthy as in the USA. Neither option sits well with the Northern ideal of warriorship.

As spiritual warriors, we must be aware of the wider society in which we live. This necessarily involves a measure of elitism. There is always some difficulty in becoming a wolf in a land of sheep. In order to function effectively, we must to some extent remain in sheep's clothing.

---

[32] Hávamál verse 80, my translation

As you progress, you may become disgusted and demoralised at the utter lack of honour, perception, and fortitude of the average citizen. This is a difficult stage to pass through. One must be mindful of the fact that they have not had the advantage of your training or initiation. Do not be drawn into despising or pitying them. Avoid making your superiority an ego issue. Practice detachment, viewing these matters as mere facts to be aware of, with no emotional significance. Only thus will you be able to remain both cheerful and honourable.

It is important that we regain some of our tribal identity to foster the initiatory process of coming into our own adulthood. While it is possible to follow the path alone, it is much more difficult. If we can provide some of our descendants with a sense of honour and identity, we will have done well. As warriors, we need to create that for ourselves.

The final step in becoming a warrior is most difficult to describe, and even more difficult to attain. Once achieved, it is easy to lapse back into the dull, confused, and fearful state which characterises the 'normal' human being. However, once on the path, the consequences of such a lapse become increasingly destructive.

The state of true warriorship is characterised by paradox. Combat without conflict. Innocence without ignorance. Discipline without effort. Grim sense of humour. The rune Dagaz is well placed as the final stage before attaining our inheritance, Othala.

In Dagaz, extremes are experienced and opposites reconciled. Truth lies in experience, not in simple logic. We can come to appreciate opposing viewpoints without being drawn into logical or emotional conflict. This leaves us free to act from an intuitive sense of rightness.

The real learning involves unlearning. Preconceptions are necessary for the novice as an easy way to deal with life's complexities, but for the warrior they are merely fetters and baggage. Giving up cherished preconceptions is not easy. It is a long and painful process. You may become negative and cynical for a while. You may be tempted to quit.

Giving up at this stage is not uncommon and leads to a state of permanent cynicism and self-interested aggressiveness. With the support of our kindred, however, we can go beyond scepticism.

Those who commonly call themselves sceptics are in fact usually just as dogmatic, intolerant, fanatical, arbitrary, evangelical, and closed minded as any fundamentalist Kristjan. They have merely exchanged one philosophical straightjacket for another. Although it must be admitted that science is at least a lot more useful and consistent than any religious dogma, sceptics need to realise that no theory can be proven, only accepted until disproved.

The Odinnic warrior can laugh at both sides. By questioning all, we become free to experience truths beyond the imagination of the belief-bound. Such an idea is frightening to many. Such a warrior will certainly appear frightening also. We will always be feared and hated by the small minded, even ridiculed by the ignorant. However, we can smile. Who hears a canary chirp when ravens caw, who hears a poodle yap when wolves bay at the moon?

If we constantly review our motivations and cull those which are unworthy or unnecessary, we will become empowered and focused on the important issues. Striving for personal power is important if one is to gain a measure of control over one's life and ability to change the world. However, if done merely to feed the ego, it will only create a house of cards, doomed to collapse.

If our heritage is to survive, it must be taken seriously, and its exponents must have credibility in the wider world. This means that we must strive to be successful, productive and respected in society, while maintaining the practices and standards of our traditions. Just take a look at the image projected by most New Age and Neo-Pagan groups and ask yourself if you would employ them in senior positions in a large company.

As an engineer in one of the largest and most conservative computer companies with considerable responsibilities, I have to meet clients regularly. I have to wear a tie, but I also wear a small hammer pinned to it. I wear runic rings, and I try to practise my warriorship at all times. I have found that, if properly understood, our traditions are most compatible with success in any field.

Once successful, we need to feed some of that success back into our traditions by sponsoring study groups, events, publishing, and the supporting technology. Those who can contribute in this way are amply rewarded. There is no future in roleplaying and escapism. It is up to us to manifest our power in Midgard. As the first rune implies, our gains must be circulated. The more you put into it, the more you get out of it. Thus the kindred as a whole will prosper, and in turn help foster your path.

Although the path of true warriorship is intensely personal and individual (the sacrifice of self unto self), the real practice of warriorship can only happen within a community. This requires the contact with, and loyalty to, others of our traditions who we can call siblings.

Which brings us back to the fact that ultimately the warrior must live in the eye of paradox. At the risk of repetition, this is the essence of Odinic warriorship. Traditional while modern, independent while community minded. The realisation of paradox in all things is the dawn of warriorship. The Day once seized becomes the home and refuge of our ancestry.

# Revenge of the Master Smith

## An ancient Germanic story retold

My love is fierce

For I am the Wolf in the wild hills waiting

I sing my love to the full moon

The shorn sheep bleat their fear in the meadow

The horned goats leap high upon the crags

Pallid moonlight from my white fangs gleaming

Warns the World of my Will and Wyrd

And my love grows deeper in the limitless well

As I weave in the ways of my long dead kin

But the sheep and the goats see only my fangs

For wolves are few and their ways wild

And the sheep and goats will never know

The ineffable bliss of freedom from fear

And the genuine joy of fierce love.

# Enter the Skald

Into the court of King Eystein strode the skald, a traveler wearing a wide brimmed hat, a sky blue cloak, and a long grey beard. Despite his apparent age, he moved with the force and confidence of a strong young warrior. He approached the King who sat at the high seat in his wooden shingled, dragon gabled hall. The king himself was a powerful figure in his middle years. The skald bowed low.

"Greetings my lord, I am called Unfrith and I have tales to tell of long ago in return for your hospitality this night."

"Welcome Unfrith. My Jarls will much appreciate a good story tonight. You shall sit at the high table, an honored guest. You shall have the best of food, the finest mead, and a bed fit for royalty, if you will tell us your greatest tale. Tonight is the feast of Yule."

When the Jarls had arrived and toasted the health of the King and each other, the food was brought in. Outside the snow was falling. The light of day had long since faded on that shortest of short northern winter days.

The King stood, a golden mead horn in his hand. "I welcome once again my loyal Jarls to Fokstua hall this Yule. I have also an unexpected guest, Unfrith here has offered to be our skald tonight."

There was a cheer from the Jarls seated at long tables either side of a central fire pit. Unfrith smiled and finished his meal, then, refilling his mead horn, he stood and raised his arms. There was an expectant silence.

"My lords, I have received here such hospitality as I have seldom before encountered. I shall tell you a tale which you have all heard before, but you shall now hear it as you have never heard it."

Another cheer went up, and then silence as the audience of noble warriors was captured by the spell of scenes of ancient times, before the Angles and Saxons settled on England's soil. The Skald told the tale of the greatest of smiths.

# Ch 1
# King Wada's Hall

It seemed as if the world wept as the rain drummed its incessant beat upon the wooden hall of King Wada. It was spring in the land of the Finns and the weather was getting warmer. The weight of Kingship bore heavily upon Wada but he was a just and conscientious ruler, and this had earned him the love and respect of his people, which he valued more than any dragon's hoard. But the King had his own hoard none the less, and of all his treasures his favourites were those wrought by the Royal Master Smith.

The smith was a Jute of great size, he wore a red beard and an almost permanent expression of detached amusement. His name was Geir which means spear, the weapon sacred to Wotan, and indeed he was a devotee of that mysterious god. Upon his massive arms were many scars, cut and coloured to form runes of power. He had married a local seeress and it had not been long before his talents in magic and metals were discovered by the King.

The royal appointment suited Geir, his only aim was to practice and perfect his skills, and this suited the King also. For many years now, barely a day had passed without the roar of the great forge bellows and the clanking of busy hammers forming objects of power and beauty from the shapeless ingots.

King Wada walked slowly to the doorway and looked out into the gathering mirk. Somewhere beyond the heavy clouds the sun was setting. As he peered though the curtain of rain, he could just make out firelight issuing from small gaps in the many houses nearby, and beyond them the bright orange glow of the forge. Even above the noise of the rain, its familiar sounds could be heard.

He was deep in thought, it would soon be time to send his three eldest sons on an expedition to prove themselves worthy of noble status. Egil, Slagfid, and Weland were now strapping youths, trained in arms and well able to look after themselves. Weland in particular was strong and wise beyond his years, he had apprenticed himself to Geir and had seven years of training in smithing and magic to fortify his body and his mind.

As a young boy, Weland had always been enchanted by the Master Smith and his creations. As soon as he was big enough to wield the smallest hammer, he started spending most of his time learning what he could from the enigmatic Jute. Geir, seeing natural ability at work, agreed to initiate Weland into the mysteries of his craft.

Weland's training had been hard work from the start. For the first year he was treated as menial labour, despite his high birth. Many times he thought about giving it up, but as he pumped the bellows or carried the ingots or fetched the water for the quenching trough, he would look at the smith and see the serene power and consummate skill. Something within Weland would not allow him to give up.

In the second year he began to learn the Runes, how to carve them and how to color them, their names and their sounds. He meditated morning and evening before meals, and followed the thought of the sound of the Ice rune back to its origin within him. After a few months he glimpsed true silence and true power. The smith told him of the gods and the many orders of beings, those which were helpful and those which were harmful.

In the third year he learned how to breathe and intone the Runes so that he perceived their force echoing throughout nature. He learned of the beings who's aid he must enlist as a smith. Geir showed him the postures used to concentrate the essence of a rune within, and the combat forms which utilized this essence. He also learned the secret lore of metals.

The next few years brought Weland the knowledge of bindrunes, he created cunningly wrought objects of power, he mastered the visualization and use of a vortex of helical force around his body to defeat his opponents in combat practice. Geir's wife, Heyd, taught him how to scry in a pot filled with spring water, how to sit out at night and converse with strange entities, and how to sing himself into a vision trance while seated on a high platform. By his eighteenth year he was a formidable warrior, a promising magician, and an extremely skilful craftsman.

On this dim, wet, northern day Weland was preparing a parting gift for his father, a gold arm ring, its ends, twined serpents heads fighting, their eyes, garnets glowing with vital force. On the inner side, bindrunes of power and protection were carved, and the glittering gold seemed to shine with an otherworldly light.

Satisfied with his creation, Weland showed it to Geir, and seeing the approval in the smith's eyes, said "You have taught me well, but one day I will match you, or maybe even better you."

The smith replied with a fond smile. "I hope so, but darkness has fallen and we should both be off home."

Weland tidied and secured the smithy, then threw about himself a huge bearskin cloak and trudged through the rain to his father's hall. There he found the King waiting, lines of care etched upon his face. "Weland, tomorrow you must prepare for the journey. It has been decided that you will go with your brothers and sail northward keeping the land ever to your right. You will come to the land of the Nomads at the northernmost end of the sea, speak with their healer, and learn whatever he will teach you. Do not tarry too long, for you must spend the next two winters in the wilderness, the healer will direct you to the place. Then you may return with stories of your adventures and be welcomed as a warrior."

"Sire, I have long awaited this day and I am glad of the adventure, but I know that I will long for the familiar faces, and the forests and lakes, and the generous embraces of our maidens. I have made a gift for you that part of me will remain here."

Weland drew the ring from beneath the wet bearskin cloak and held it before his father's captured gaze. "My son, seldom have I seen such a treasure, our master smith would be hard put to equal this."

Weland looked down at the puddle of water which had dripped from his clothes since he entered. "It will be many years before I can match his subtlety."

Wada gazed long at the ring, turning it in his hands. "I will wear it always. I know it will give me strength in an hour of need." He placed it upon his arm, a snug fit around his bicep. The serpents seemed to writhe and bite as the gold glittered in the firelight.

That night Weland retired early and spent much of the evening thinking of all that he had learned, and how much more he wanted to learn. He felt a little annoyed at having to disrupt his studies, yet he couldn't help feeling excited about the prospect of an adventure. He sank into a deep slumber, from the depths of which strange visions arose and he found himself in a vivid dream.

He saw about him soldiers with steel helmets and sharp swords, he was bound and could not move. Cold and cruel, the face of an aristocratic woman appeared before him. Cold and cruel, her laughter rang in his ears. A searing pain tore at the back of his right leg. He convulsed, instantly awake, the scream ripped from his throat muffled by the bearskins into which his face was pressed. His right hamstring muscle knotted in an agony of cramp. Through the pain and sweat, he saw between the hides which hung across his window, a full moon high in the western sky. In the distance, the sound of a pack of wolves howling. The cramp passed quickly and Weland drifted into a dreamless sleep.

When he awoke it was after dawn and the sun was bright upon the newly washed forests and fields. Weland's morning meditation was forced and broken, he did not even attempt his usual exercises in runic postures and breathing. He had a hurried breakfast and made his way to the smithy. There he found the Master waiting for him.

"It is unlike you, Weland, to arrive so late in the morning, and wearing such a troubled look."

"As much as I am looking forward to this adventure, I cannot be confident about my return."

"A portent?" The smith's great brows were knitted with concern.

"My dreams of late have revealed to me a deadly witch. I have heard her laughter in the howling of wolves, in the cracking of stones in the night's frost, like a dagger of ice. If I meet her I will become her prisoner."

"You have glimpsed your wyrd, there is no escaping it, even the gods are subject to the wyrd that they weave. But do not forget that you are weaving it with every thought and action. Ultimately you are responsible for it, and you are its master."

"What then of the norns, have they no hand in this?" Weland was clutching at straws.

"Never seek to blame your situation on anything other than your own actions. There are those who blame the norns for their misfortunes, or they blame the King, or their enemies, even their friends. A warrior must accept responsibility for his life, only thus can he take control of it. Even an act of revenge must be purely to redress the balance of your wyrd, not to put blame on your enemy.

"The norns weave the web blindly according to the dictates of the web of which they too are part. The three Norns are the guardians of the three states of existence within the web which contains all.

"Urd is the keeper of the well of all possibilities. Her name means 'primal', in her realm reside all that is unmanifest or not known to us.

"Skuld, who's name means 'should' is involved with all that is known only by inference. We can say what should happen tomorrow if our information is correct, or if our divination is skilful. But we all have free will and can choose to change the course of events, thus she is called 'should' and not 'shall'. We can never be certain about this realm, we can only say what should be, or what should have been, according to our incomplete evidence. Most of our world resides in this realm, and all of the future.

"Then there is Verdandi, who's name means 'the unfolding World'. Her realm is the manifesting world. Which brings us back to where we are now."

Weland did not move or speak for a long time. He felt as though a great revelation were about to descend upon him. This explanation of the Norns was new to him, and it seemed that much of that which he did not understand in his training were about to fall into place. When he looked at Geir, he saw the amused and enigmatic expression which usually accompanied a good riddle.

The next two days were taken up with preparations for the voyage. A sturdy boat was prepared and laden with provisions. The craft was blessed and sacrifices were made to the sea gods. A great feast was held and there were many toasts to the three brothers, Weland, Egil, and Slagfid. After the feast all three found most pleasing company waiting when they retired to their beds.

## Ch 2
## The Journey

The sun seemed to shine a little too brightly for three young men slightly the worst for wear after several drinking horns of mead the night before. The brothers, equiped with swords, shields, and helmets, certainly looked the equal of any adventure, but King Wada knew that the lands beyond his small kingdom were strange and dangerous. This test was no mere token.

The three brothers strode proudly to the nearby beach where the small square-rigged craft lay ready, its bow resting upon the shore and its stern nudged by the breaking waves. The whole town had come out to see them go, forming a rather informal procession behind them. After many hugs and pats on the back, and a brief speech from the king, the brothers started stowing the last of their provisions. Weland felt a huge hand rest upon his shoulder, he turned, knowing well its owner. Geir stood silent, a wordless look of understanding passing between them, he extended the hilt of a magnificent sword toward Weland, who unbuckled his own and strapped the gift to his side. Its jeweled pommel glittered, Weland longed to draw the blade from its scabbard, but now was not the time. Geir spoke.

"This is the blade which you forged, tempered, and sharpened with such care, it was to be for the Captain of the Kings Guard but I can make him another. It is best to wear a weapon of your own making, if you have trust in your skill. I have made a hilt and pommel in deer-antler and silver to match the workmanship of the steel."

Weland knew he had a blade on which he could depend, and as he felt the boat slide free of the beach, preparing to take them into the unknown, he was much heartened to feel the reassuring weight at his side.

There was just enough breeze to spare them from having to row, and with Egil at the steering board they proceeded northward at a leisurely pace. The waving and shouting of their friends was soon lost in the distance. They had no idea how far the northern end of the sea was, except that it would take many days to get there. The days were long and getting longer at that time of year and they could make good progress if the weather held out. With the sun behind them and keeping sight of the shore to their right, the brothers found themselves still in familiar territory at the end of the day.

A little more than a ten league ride to the north of their home was the estate of one of their uncles. Not long before sunset they found an inlet and rowed about half a league inland. As they tied the boat to the wharf and approached the small group of houses, they could smell the evening meal cooking.

The sound of barking dogs suddenly filled the air and helmetted bowmen could be seen running from the main hall and vanishing into the surrounding woods. Egil took a hunting horn from his belt and blew the family hunting tune. Uncle Atli was always well prepared and the brothers realised that they should have blown the horn before they moored the boat, this mistake could have been their last. The Niars from the other side of the narrow sea had often raided homesteads, sailing up the inlets and attacking without warning, usually at dusk. The time of day and the direction of their approach had certainly given their uncle's people cause for alarm.

At the sound of the familiar tune, the bowmen paused long enough to see that there were only three warriors, but their deadly shafts were ready and the occasional rustling was the only sign that they were keeping well within range. Atli was standing at the doorway of the hall, flanked by several men with spears.

"Three young boars thought they would like to join our sow on the spit." Uncle Atli was not tall but he was heavily built and strong, he was wearing his usual manic grin and his arms were held wide in greeting. In his youth he had traveled widely, he knew more about other lands and peoples than anyone else the brothers could think of. Atli was respected and feared, on his travels he had learned the art of berserk, but his grin alone was enough to unnerve a seasoned warrior.

"Good Uncle, is there room at your table for three travellers." Weland yelled loudly in case any of the unseen bowmen did not yet realise their identity.

"There is always room for travellers at my board, my hospitality is legend. The more so for my own kin." Atli replied even more loudly, aware that his men were well trained in silent death and invisible in the gathering darkness. The three found themselves suddenly surrounded by the familiar faces of Earl Atli's household, the bowmen had appeared like phantoms. With many greetings and a good deal of mirth, they all entered the hall.

There was not much that one could call orthodox about Atli, some called him eccentric. The way he trained his men, the exotic hangings in his hall, some quite tarnished by smoke haze from the fire pit, his sense of humour in particular, all bespoke the influence of strange lands. It was his knowledge of other places that most interested the brothers, and after a generous horn-full of a particularly good local mead, Atli's knowledge flowed forth.

Tales of people with strange looks and customs held the guests spellbound for hours. Travelling with a group of Saxon mercenaries, Atli had seen huge towns in the south where houses were made with stones of baked clay and sometimes had second floors where the rooves should have been.

Weland always enjoyed Atli's tales, but at one point he began to feel quite uneasy. He had been in a jovial mood until then, appreciating the company, the food, and the comfort of the mead hall. Atli was speaking of the Niars less than one hundred miles west across the sea. Despite their closeness, not a great deal was known about them. They came to raid the smaller coastal settlements at times but otherwise kept very much to themselves. Atli had, however, captured one some years before. The man had served him well as a slave and Atli had recently set him free. The man had told Atli of King Nidhad who's queen ruled him and his kingdom with her cunning. He told also of the Kings counsellor who hated the queen but feared her more, and so acted as her puppet. Weland shuddered slightly, not certain whether the chill on his spine was due to a stray draught or to the feeling of unease which he knew to be a warning of danger to come.

That night everyone slept well, but long before dawn Weland half woke to the sound of a woman's laughter which rang like a dagger drawn from a jeweled scabbard. As his mind fought towards consciousness, he could hear nothing but the howling of wolves far off in the forest.

As the sun rose, casting a light of the same golden hue as the mead they had enjoyed the night before, the three brothers rowed the small craft out of the estuary and turned the prow northward. It was not long before the gusty winds had carried them almost too far from shore, but at least their progress was swift.

For the next week they saw no-one. By day they sailed and caught fish, in the evening they would come ashore and set up cow hide tents then cook their fish, and at the first light of dawn they would stow their gear and collect what nuts and berries they could find. By sunrise each day they were back on the water.

As they approached the northernmost reaches of the kingdom, it seemed to them that some strange and powerful mind had bent its will toward them. Often they would see ravens circle above them briefly and then fly northward with mournful cries, as if to herald their coming as a great misfortune. More than once they saw the grey shape of a lone wolf at dawn, although at a distance, it was clearly watching them. This in itself was nothing strange. It was most likely a different wolf each time, and lone wolves were known to scavenge at the campsites of travellers. Still, such thoughts offer no comfort when it is plain that Wyrd is at work, and to foster complacency with pale rationalisations is to invite an untimely end. The coward uses words to hide his fear even from himself, but in the end fear conquers him. The warrior faces fear and conquers it.

So it was that the brothers at last came close to the northern end of the sea, a land inhabited only by reindeer hunters. These people lived in deerhide tents and never stayed long in one place. They were known to possess few objects of metal and were thus considered poor by their more settled neighbours. Their only weapons were bows and hunting spears, their only protection from the steel swords of the warlike tribes to the south was the apparent poverty of their situation, their constant movement, and their reputation for witchcraft. These were the nomads whose aid they needed for their quest.

As the boat came to shore once more, Egil looked upon the cold and uninhabited wilderness before them. "How are we to find humans in this land, let alone a nomad healer?"

"He will find us." Weland's reply carried such conviction that his brothers could only accept it, realising that Weland had access to news from sources unknown to them.

"We had better choose our campsite carefully. Although the nomad healer knows where we are, I do not know when he will arrive. I feel that he has friendly intentions, but I also feel something here which may not appreciate our presence."

Weland's brothers gripped their sword hilts and felt the hair bristle on their necks. They too were now aware of an uneasy feeling in the air, as if the unfamiliar wilderness itself resented the tread of human feet. It watched and waited with an open malice. With two hours of light left, there was an unspoken agreement that they should be well prepared for the coming night.

# Ch3
# The Trollman

As the inky blackness pressed about them, the day's last traces fading from the western sky, the narrow sickle of the moon, just past new, could be seen, soon to sink into the whispering sea. The night would be illuminated only by the few stars winking through the patchwork of cloud. Only two weeks after leaving home, they already felt as if in another world, one inhabited by strange people and entities unknown to them. The feeling of disquiet became oppressive.

After a meal of fresh fish, more pieces of driftwood were thrown on the fire. The little circle of dancing yellow light offered some comfort, but the shadows that each cast as he huddled close to the fire, made bizarre shapes which seemed to jump and lunge at them from the impenetrable darkness of the wild land surrounding them.

They decided to keep watch during the night and drew lots to determine which hours each should stand guard. Egil took the first shift while the others retired to get as much rest as they could before their turns came. He turned his rugged features inland, where the uneasy feeling was strongest, drew his sword, and sat with his back to the fire.

A little after midnight Weland awoke from a short and tormented sleep. The vivid dream images, still fresh in his mind, made no sense to him. His fear, however, was real enough. It was something he had never before experienced. Something in the back of his mind was stirring, as if from a lightless pit. A force so powerful and so alien, he fought for self control. Only his years of hard discipline at Geir's forge prevented him from releasing the insane scream which tore at his throat. He could accept death at the hand of an enemy, or deep in the cold seas. He believed that there was a part of him which nothing could touch, until now.

"Weland, your watch." Egil whispered.

Hiding his terror, Weland pretended to wake from a deep sleep.

"All well?" He asked with a yawn, a little too casually.

"I don't like it. It's just too quiet."

"You should sleep well then." Weland's jest fell flat, but, he reflected that at least he could be thankful that Egil did not perceive whatever it was that was even now rushing like a huge black wave to crash down and engulf him utterly.

He was not long on watch when Weland felt the hair on the back of his neck prickle. He was being watched. His first reaction was to put more wood on the fire. The resulting light only made it harder to see anything in the shadows and, he suddenly realised, easier for him to be seen by anything out there. He cursed his helplessness, a short rasp escaping from his throat, a sound which he felt only drew this demon closer. He suspected from the many tales he had heard, that this was the presence of a troll. Few had ever escaped from one alive, fewer still sane.

Panicking he kicked the main log out of the fire, sending up a shower of sparks as the smaller sticks and embers flew about. The flames died out rapidly, and the pitch darkness drew in around him like a garrotte around the neck of a sacrificial prisoner.

Transfixed, his mind tumbled. Even his mad scream found no escape, but crashed and echoed through his brain, while barely a hiss issued from his knotted throat.

The troll was before him, a darker patch of black against the blind darkness around him. Tendrils of cold lashed from it, seeking the intruder. Weland's mind was lost in sheer terror, engulfed in utter madness and chaos. Weland had almost abandoned himself to absolute insanity and complete destruction, when something within him, some small sheltered space within the maelstrom of his mind, gave him just enough pause to draw his sword.

The act itself empowered him. He shook off the paralysis, replacing confusion with cold rage. Knowing that his foe was likely to be devoid of physical form, he raised his sword high above his head and charged it with magickal intent. Marshaling the full force of his will, Weland brought the great blade around in a wide arc, searing the troll with its flashing power.

A fierce blast of wind sprang up suddenly, sending him sprawling. The wind roared as if the land itself gave voice to its contempt. Struggling to regain his feet, Weland realised that he was no match for this fiend. It was merely playing with him.

Mentally preparing himself for death, the young prince searched his mind for any advice on combat. Geir's words came to him. "Become as one with your enemy, possess not hate, possess not anger, they will only defeat you. Become as the berserk, without shield or armour, open your breast to the foe. Move as water, resist nothing, you will be no longer a target. Let the enemy destroy himself, or become your friend."

Uncle Atli had learned the art. He had once explained that without armour the berserk is faster and more flexible. As he wades though a sea of blades, being one with the battle, the berserk flows, seemingly impervious to steel. Where a blade strikes, he is not. So it was with fierce joy that Atli lived, and with fierce joy he would die.

Mustering his whole will, Weland became silent. He cast aside layer after layer of thoughts, ideas, perceptions, leaving his mind naked and transparent before the immense lashing and crackling of unimaginable power which played around the troll. Then he made contact.

Although, as if in curiosity, the troll seemed to become quieter, Weland felt an enormous surge of power through his body. The force was beyond anything he had ever imagined, he felt that he was about to faint. From the edge of unconsciousness he became aware that this experience was overwhelming only because of his automatic resistance to it. He relaxed and accepted the force without resistance and found that he was immediately fully conscious again.

He was aware now of the nature of the being whose energy flowed through him. It was ancient, truly a part of this wild and desolate land. It had no physical form but its gender was feminine. He could feel empathically everything that it was feeling. It was a solitary creature, at one with the land but whose experience with other sentient beings had been limited to the destruction of humans who blundered along occasionally and upset the serenity of the land.

This was the first time any other mind had opened itself to her, she was surprised and curious. She could feel everything that it felt, and she knew that this awareness was mutual. She found the experience pleasurable. Deep within her some instinct, almost lost in the depths of time, drew her and comforted her, but at the same time excited her.

The lashing tendrils of wild energy started to play about her once more, but this time they did not threaten, they caressed.

Weland felt his own energy form similar tendrils which began to intertwine with hers. He was more aware of this energy body now than his physical one and threw off his clothes with contempt. The feeling of the twining, caressing energy became clearer and its pitch seemed to rise.

The troll saw Weland form his energy body to become more salient to her. She in turn started to manifest a physical body for him to more easily perceive her. Within the crackling field of energy a faintly glowing shape started to form. It soon took on the aspect of a woman, her features bizarre but beautiful. The forces which danced around them whipped into a higher pitch again and continued increasing as their two physical bodies came together and entwined in a passionate embrace.

The wind started to howl once more, and great bolts of lightning smote the ground around them as they writhed together, their energy thrashing wildly. The tempest raged ever more fiercely as Weland's brothers could only shelter beneath hides. Its climax uprooted trees and shook the rocks in the ground. Then it passed and silence reigned once more.

They lay together for a short time and then the troll's physical form faded and her energy body poured itself back into the earth, returning to her home. He could feel, however, that she had left him with substantial power, a priceless gift.

Weland found himself sitting alone on the beach some distance from the camp. He could hear his brothers calling for him and could see that they had just rebuilt the fire. He called back to them.

When Slagfid and Egil ran to find him, each holding a lighted brand against the darkness, they found him sitting on the beach wearing nothing but a wide grin. Cautious, fearing that they may well be confronting a madman, Slagfid asked, "We feared that the wind may have blown you a fair distance, but this is the first time I have seen a wind strip all the clothes off a man."

Weland laughed, but it was not the laugh of the insane. He stood up and slapped them both on the back. They walked briskly back to camp and Weland found his clothes only a few paces from the fire. Only then did he start to feel the chill of the night air. As he dressed himself he told the others that he had placated the land spirit and there would be no further danger.

They listened and heard the familiar night sounds. The mood had changed completely, they now felt quite at ease. As they drifted off to sleep, each had the distinct impression that the land itself held him safely in its palm. No harm would come to them this night. Even their dreams where of the most pleasant kind.

When at last they awoke, the sun was already well over the eastern hills. They sat up with a start when they heard a strangely accented voice greeting them.

"Hail Slagfid, prince among Finns."

"Hail Egil, prince among Finns."

"Hail Weland, prince among Finns, and trollman honoured among us."

# Ch 4
# The Nomads

Before the brothers, stood a man of outlandish appearance. His face was tanned and deeply lined, his hair was pitch black. His features reminded them of a trader from the eastern lands they had once seen at Atli's hall. His clothes were just as strange to them, clad from head to foot in furs, his boots had upturned toes. He wore a wolfskin headdress, the wolf's head upon his, with amber set into the eye sockets. The amber eyes looked very realistic, glittering as he moved. A cape of raven's feathers hung from his shoulders. Weland knew at once that this was the healer they sought.

"We have walked for many days to meet you. The deer herds are many leagues to the north at present. My messengers have told me of your progress. I am known to your wise ones as Kveld"

They remembered the wolves and ravens which had seemed to watch them. They became aware also of several other nomads seated quietly nearby, dressed similarly in furs but without headgear or cape.

"I feared that I may not reach you in time, this area can be dangerous to strangers. It is a wonder indeed that you were accepted by the spirits here." With this he looked directly at Weland and smiled. Weland wondered how much the healer knew, but felt comfortable if he should know all.

"We made camp last night about five hours walk to the north. Come there with us, it is more sheltered, let us give you what hospitality we have until you must leave. Tell me how your father fares, I have not seen him for many years."

When the Brothers had stowed their boat and possessions safely among some trees, the party set off northward. Although small of stature, Kveld and his men lead at a pace rather faster than the brothers were used to, and were soon quite a distance from the sea. They slowed down a little when Kveld noticed that his questions were being answered in gasps.

When they reached the campsite it was late afternoon, two hunters were already preparing their evening meal. They sat down around the fire and Kveld turned to Weland.

"My friend Geir has sent me a message. He would like you to learn about the Yrminsul. That is his word for the world column, the axis which joins the various realms of being, the trunk of the world tree. You will need to be away from others for one month, your brothers can stay here. There is a valley not far from here, we will set up a tent there."

The brothers were happy to stay a while with the friendly nomads, the tents were more roomy and comfortable than their own. Weland was intrigued that the nomads possessed no objects of metal except for a few small steel knives. He learned that they had no knowledge of metalwork, the prized blades had been bought from tribes to the south in exchange for hides. The heads of their spears and arrows were cunningly made from very sharp flakes of stone or carved from antler with barbs for catching fish. Every tool they needed could be fashioned from stone, antler or bone. All of their other possessions were made from wood, deer hide, or the skins of wild animals. Some considered them poor, but Weland could see that they were able to live comfortably without help from anyone else, and without the need for craftsmen like himself. Their independence gave them an air of self confidence which he admired. They seemed at one with the land in which they lived.

After a simple meal, they retired to their beds early. They slept more soundly and more peacefully than they had since they were children.

At first light they awoke refreshed to find the nomads already at breakfast. Kveld greeted them and motioned Weland to sit beside him.

"We shall go to the valley when you have eaten. Two of my men shall help carry the things we will need."

As the first golden rays of the sun speared between the hills, the healer and the prince set off. Walking toward the rising sun, they reached the valley well before noon. Among birch and pine Weland's tent was set, and then he was left alone with Kveld.

"First you must prepare for the journey, you must do this alone. I will only be here when it is necessary, but I will camp not too far away. You must follow my instructions exactly or you may find yourself in great danger. It is fortunate that you have trained with Geir, he will have taught you the discipline you will need.

"For the next two weeks you will eat only the little food that I bring you. You must be purified before you approach that tree, the mighty Yrminsul. Only then may you summon the Eagle and climb to the realms of the gods or descend with the Serpent to the world of the dead and the land spirits and elves. More important than the journey is the returning, for that is where the true centre lies, on this the middle-world."

Some of this seemed familiar to Weland but most of it was strange. He looked forward to the challenge he was facing, although he felt it would be his most difficult one. Kveld, sensing Weland's mood, became stern.

"If you have any doubts, let us return. I can point you in the right direction to continue your test."

"I Wish to learn whatever you will teach me." Weland's reply was quiet but resolute. Kveld smiled.

"I think you will be a worthy student. Let us begin by making your tomb."

For the next three days Weland toiled. Under Kveld's direction, he built, with stones and branches, a small chamber just large enough for him to lie down in. Then a long curved passage through which he could only just crawl. The whole structure was then covered with earth except for the end away from the entrance, this was covered with layers of stones and pine needles. When he had finished, he felt weak from hunger and exertion.

For the next nine days Weland sat alone in his tent meditating, except for the daily meal of nuts and berries Kveld brought him. The healer would arrive at dawn each day with the food and a lesson, he would leave well before noon. Weland learned a chant to call forth his spirit helpers, he learned that he would need to rise from the grave healed, he would need the protection of his allies before he could attempt the Tree. Little by little he was made ready.

After the nine days it was time to enter the tomb. Kveld would wait near the entrance, in Weland's tent. His only instructions were to remain until he was given a sign to bring back. Kveld opened a bag and took out a necklace made of human finger bones carved into the shape of skulls. He hung it carefully around Weland's neck and demonstrated a chant to call the spirits. Weland entered the tomb chanting.

The air in the chamber had an earthy smell. The stones and pine needles allowed a slight movement of air but admitted no light or sound. As Weland continued the chant, his mind began to feel numb, he lost all sense of time. Pinpoint flashes of light began to appear before his eyes, then starbursts, and at length swirling patterns. He noticed that he had stopped chanting, whether for an hour or a week he could not tell.

With an effort he started chanting, concentrating on calling the spirits, it seemed endless. In the patterns of light which danced before him, whether his eyes were open or closed, he started to see faces forming. Pale ghosts and demons with pointed teeth. They were gibbering in some strange tongue but it was obvious that they were planning a banquet.

His defenceless body felt leaden. The demons rushed at him. Suddenly he was viewing the scene from above. With total detachment, he watched as his lifeless body was dismembered, his flesh devoured, and his bones broken. He felt strangely free. He was very tempted to just fly away leaving his body to rot, but he had a task to complete.

In his detached state, he found it difficult to feel any sense of purpose. Summoning his will, he bent his concentration back upon the creatures he had called.

"I have given myself freely, which of you shall give me help and protection from this day forward."

All but two of the spirits vanished. Weland found himself looking at an enormous striped cat with teeth like daggers and a human shape about two feet tall who's skin and clothes were utterly black, even its eyes were like polished spheres of obsidian.

"Give me proof that you two are indeed my helpers."

The man in black laughed. "Behold the Guardian of the Sacred Tree of Knowledge."

Weland was suddenly witnessing a snow scene across which a sled raced at terrific speed, it was pulled by reindeer. He did not understand the significance of this, the nomads often used sleds, but pulled them by hand and did not harness animals. As it came nearer, he could see that it carried an old man who was laughing, something about the old man was quite bizarre, he did not look at all like a nomad.

Just as suddenly, he was back with his helpers. "I will have to take your word that this will provide proof, but now how will I get myself back together?"

The man in black drew a glowing rune in the air. "Heal thyself, smith, in the forge of thyself. Make sure the fire is hot enough."

Weland recognised the rune called 'kenaz', the torch, but also the fire of the forge. Invoking the force of the rune, he felt every fibre of his being starting to burn. A chant came to his voice unbidden. It was the chant he had learned from Geir to help with the rhythmic pumping of the forge bellows. He felt himself glowing red, then orange, then yellow. Finally, blinded by the brightness of white heat and deafened by the roar of a thousand forges. He returned to the darkness and silence of the tomb.

Emerging from the mouth of the grave, his eyes blinking against the light, the young smith was glad that Kveld was there to offer his strange midwifery.

"How long was I in there?"

"Only two days, you are lucky. The sun is about to rise, a good omen. Now I shall ask the questions."

Kveld insisted on hearing every detail. When it came to the part about the helper's proof, he became even more attentive, his eyes opened wide.

"The reindeer sled is significant, tell me about the old man."

"He was dressed as a nomad except in two respects, his furs were colorful, and he wore a long beard. Are there such people known to you?"

"There are none in these lands who fit that description. We do not wear beards or color our furs."

"And I know of no other people who use reindeer sleds."

"It certainly sounds like the Guardian of the Tree of Knowledge, but to be sure, I must know what colors he wore."

"His beard was white and his furs were red-gold with white patches."

Kveld took a large mushroom from his bag and held it up. "Like these colors?"

"Precisely those." Weland stared at the fungus in amazement. It had a thick white stem and a fleshy red-gold cap with small white patches. Even its shape reminded him of the old man in the sled, rather fatter than any nomad he had seen.

Weland had seen the fungus many times in his own country, it was known as a poison and often used to attract and kill flies. He turned to the healer with a puzzled look.

"What is the Tree of Knowledge, Kveld?"

"This." Kveld held up the mushroom again. "It will help you find the World Tree. You saw the Guardian, it was a great omen. Your spirit helpers were genuine and you are favoured by the Tree."

"What would have happened if I had not found my helpers?"

Kveld answered with a smile and a casual shrug. "You would have died."

# Ch 5
# The Yrminsul

For the next few days Weland was given enough food to recover his strength. Kveld moved his tent to a spot within sight of Weland's. More detailed instructions on chanting and power dances were given. The importance of the ritual drum was made clear.

Kveld Showed Weland a drum made from a hoop of wood with a skin stretched over it, he had a stick with a rounded end as a beater. Its tone was surprisingly low and booming. This he gave to Weland. He then took out his own drum and taught a rapid beat.

At first Weland found the drumming tiring, his arms would become tired and cramped after a few minutes while Kveld seemed tireless. Yet Weland was accustomed to wielding heavy hammers all day at the forge, it frustrated him to tire from such a light task.

"You have too much tension in the shoulders, relax. Watch." Kveld doubled the pace without effort, his hand a blur. No sign of strain could be seen. Weland could feel the reverberations through his body, he started to feel light headed, it seemed as if the drum was trying to pull him out of his body through the top of his head. Kveld stopped abruptly. "You must practice until the drum seems to play itself."

Four days later the apprentice was able to keep up a reasonable beat for more than an hour without having to concentrate. While Weland practiced, Kveld started to prepare a mixture of water, herbs, and juice from the mushroom, explaining that the juice could indeed be deadly if not prepared in exactly the right way. Uttering a different incantation at each stage of the process, Kveld soon had a bowl of liquid which he covered and put in the shade.

"At dusk you shall start your journey. Rest until then." Kveld continued with the preparations until late in the afternoon.

When it was nearly sunset, the healer led the apprentice to a nearby clearing in which a large circle was marked out with stones. At the centre stood a plain wooden pole about ten feet high. Kveld entered the circle and placed the bowl of juices near the base of the pole. He then danced around the circle beating his drum and lighting a fire at each of the four directions while chanting. He motioned Weland to follow, he repeated the dance.

Returning to the centre, Kveld picked up the bowl and held it aloft intoning a long prayer to several deities. He turned to Weland and gave him the bowl. Weland paused briefly to incant a formula, it was for the blessing of Wotan in the search for knowledge. "And sacrificed Wotan himself unto himself." He drank the brew, the drumming began.

With a whirling dance the two drummers set up a steady booming. They continued for quite some time, Kveld pausing occasionally to feed the quarter fires. It was dark and the firelight made the healer appear even more otherworldly than usual. Weland whirled and drummed tirelessly, he felt himself grinning. It was indeed as if the drum played of its own volition.

Weland's mind lurched as he suddenly noticed that he was now taking rather large steps over logs and stones which were not there before. He looked again and found that they were really only sticks and pebbles. He knew that he must start calling his spirit helpers before the strange brew worked its full effect, lest he lose control and end up lost in the spirit worlds.

As if by instinct his dance became ferocious and catlike, he could sense the striped creature approaching. It danced with him in the circle. After a while it sat near the base of the pole and Weland's dance became more bizarre. With stiff hopping movements, the small man in black came to the dance.

By now the division between middle world and spirit world had dissolved. None of the objects within view had any perspective or proportion. Size ceased to have meaning. Weland could not tell whether Kveld was the size of a mountain or an ant, he seemed both.

The drumming became faster and louder and Weland felt again that it was pulling him out of himself through the top of his head. He did not fight it. He was briefly aware of two figures drumming in the circle, then he left his body still drumming. Now in his spirit body, with his helpers on either side, he turned to the centre.

There stood a gigantic column, the trunk of a tree who's lowest branches were too high to be visible. He called to the

Eagle. There was a deafening eagle cry and he was catapulted at blinding speed into the realm of the gods.

He saw beings of great beauty, power and wisdom. It seemed that he himself was shining. They seemed to have everything and yet they were not quite complete. As he tried to understand why he felt this, two figures came toward him. He recognised them as Wotan and Freya.

"I sent you the man in black." Wotan's single eye blazed with power and knowledge. "He will help you find those things most carefully hidden, but beware his sense of humor."

"I sent you the cat." Freya's voice was like music, it enchanted and caressed. Love in all of its manifestations seemed to pour from her. " She will help you to make your every act an act of love."

Weland pondered for a brief moment and replied. "I thank you Lord and Lady." He wondered what the Serpent had in store.

The instant the thought entered his mind, he found himself plummeting at great speed down a tube within the trunk of the Tree. He was ejected suddenly into a dark realm of ghosts and demons. He felt somehow that his own appearance had become demonic. Through the mist two monstrous beings approached, he recognised them as Loki and Hel.

"I sent you the man in black." Loki was pale, as if he had not seen daylight for many aeons. He sneered in disdain. "He will kick your backside when you get too big for your boots. Trust him with your life."

"I sent you the cat." Hel's face was a sickly blue and the odour of corpses wafted from her. "She will claw your face if you let emotion rule you."

Weland thought briefly, and replied. "Surely you lie, the Eagle vision....".

Before he could finish, he was once again shot up to the top of the Tree and stood rather unsteadily before Wotan and Freya. Wotan's one eye glittered, his expression, a permanent knowing wink. Weland was confused, the gods started to laugh.

"In the Serpent realm they said....." Suddenly Weland was dragged back down to stand wobbling before Loki and Hel. They were laughing. He turned to the man in black. "What is the truth."

"Nothing is true." The man in black stared at him with his large, expressionless, black orbs.

"But that's not possible!" Weland was starting to panic, his exclamation merely giving voice to his desire for answers that he could understand.

"Everything is possible." The man in black stared at him with eyes which showed no whites, nor was there any iris visible. The eyes were just two huge pupils.

"How do I get back to the Middle-World."

"Balance." The man in black did not seem very helpful.

Weland thought of the Eagle force, and was once more propelled upward. Again amongst the near-hysterical gods, he became aware of the Eagle and Serpent forces pulling him in opposite directions. His thoughts caused the balance to shift, sending him hurtling from one world to the other. "Balance!" he exclaimed.

While holding the Eagle force in his mind, he slowly increased his image of the Serpent. They were almost balanced when he was suddenly hurled into the Nether-World again. He needed a new approach.

Weland closed his eyes. He slowly drew the Eagle force down through the top of his head, while at the same time drawing the Serpent force up through his feet. He visualised the energies stopping at certain points and reaching a new equilibrium, then continuing until at last coming together at his solar plexus.

There was a flash like lightning and Weland felt the two forces become one. The new force was entirely of his own nature. He was now complete in a way that neither the gods nor the demons had been. He opened his eyes to find himself back in the circle, still drumming, with Kveld beside him.

The nomad grinned at him. "You are now a healer."

They danced again around the circle thanking the four quarters, and the gods, and the demons, then went to their beds and slept.

Early the following morning, they were joined at breakfast by the two nomad helpers. When their things were packed they set off for the main campsite. They walked in cheerful silence, Weland could not put into words what he had learned.

Back at camp, Weland found his brothers busy carving implements and ornaments of antler and bone. "I'm glad we have all learned something here, our new skills may be very useful during our journey."

Egil and Slagfid leapt up to greet him, numerous questions came at him. The brothers were somewhat disappointed with Weland's answers at first, but Kveld explained that some things were hard to put into words, and some things were not for the ears of others. They accepted this.

Kveld looked up at the sky and seemed to sniff the air. "I will divine your direction tonight, you must leave as soon as possible and find a place to spend winter.

That night, the nomads held a parting feast for the brothers. After the meal, the healer took the shoulder blade from the deer which had been cooked for the occasion. He cleaned off all of the meat with a stone knife, uttered some prayers, and threw the bone on the fire. He watched it closely for a short time then flicked it out of the fire with a stick. He studied it intently, lines and cracks had appeared on its surface and he seemed to be reading them like a secret message. Weland could see that Kveld was reading the lines of Wyrd as they intersected that time and place.

"The way of knowledge lies southward along the Niar coast. Great is the adventure, but there will be danger. Weland will suffer most. Beware the Niara king, Nidhad, and more so his queen. Open no tombs, lest they be cursed and Wyrd turn against you."

With that, they prepared to continue their journey. After a good sleep and an early start, they reached the boat by midday. They found their possessions as they had left them and Weland rummaged though a bag to find some small knife blades that he had made with great skill at Geir's forge. These he gave to the nomads. They had never seen such workmanship in steel and were quite moved by the gift. Weland gave Kveld a silver ring carved with runes of power. He was almost embarrassed that he could not give more. "It is a small thing compared to what you have done for me."

Kveld smiled. "The value of a gift is in the reason for the giving."

Weland hoped that he would return one day, but he and his brothers were now eager to resume their quest. The boat slid easily into the lapping waves, and as if by request, a cool wind sprang up from the north.

# Ch 6
# Wolfdales

The brothers decided that, rather than following the coast around, they would risk the open sea. A south-westerly heading would take them directly to the lands they sought in about three days, saving them at least a week. The Niars in their long, sleek boats navigated the open sea with ease, raiding along the entire coastline. Weland's people did not have the skills to build such craft, nor to navigate with such accuracy.

They drew lots to organize shifts at the rudder. During the day, it would not be too difficult to keep their direction, but at night, they had to rely on Weland's intuition that the pole star would not be hidden by cloud.

The first night was indeed almost cloudless, the wind sighed softly in the sail, and the only other sound was the slapping of the waves against the boat. The second day and night were a little more cloudy, but they continued without trouble. On the third day they were expecting to sight land sometime in the afternoon, but heavy clouds were gathering and they could barely judge the direction of the sun.

By late afternoon there was still no sign of land. The moon was not due to rise until just before dawn. They had not anticipated the problem of landing the boat in the dark. The sky had become heavily overcast, nightfall was swift and the darkness total. Even the wind, their last indicator of direction, dropped to utter stillness and the sail hung limp and useless. After a while the waves no longer slapped but rocked them gently.

"We can't row, I can't even see my own hands." The voice was Egil's, it seemed small and disembodied in the thick blackness which surrounded them.

"We have no way of telling the direction. What do we do now?" Slagfid spoke a little too loudly, he had forgotten in the dark, that his brothers sat only an arms length away.

"We may as well sleep, there is nothing else we can do. I feel certain that we will sight land tomorrow." There was no argument to Weland's suggestion, they were all quite tired.

Weland's sleep was deep but disturbed. He could feel icy fingers reaching toward him, seeking his location. He heard a woman's voice, as cold and sharp as a drawn dagger. "You will work for me, smith." Her laughter pierced him like needles of ice.

When they awoke, they found their predicament was not much better. There was enough light to see each other, but a thick fog prevented them from seeing more than an oars length. There was nothing to do but wait, they returned to their slumber.

A little later, a shout from Egil woke the others. They sat up to find themselves floating in a wide inlet with steep wooded sides, they were almost surrounded by mountains. After surveying their new situation, and feeling encouraged at the sight of solid ground, they took to the oars to investigate further inland.

The estuary was wide and deep for a league or more before narrowing suddenly, becoming a fast flowing river. This halted progress upstream by boat. They stopped rowing and drifted slowly back toward the sea. Currents took the boat to the other side of the inlet. From this position a wooded knoll came into view, not far from a convenient beach. Upon that knoll was a large hut, almost hidden by a hedge of small trees.

Slagfid eyed the dwelling suspiciously, there was no sign of life. "It is either a hunting lodge or a retreat for outlaws."

Egil too, was cautious. "If we approach the hut, we may find it deserted, we may surprise the inhabitants and end up in a fight, or if they have already seen us, we could walk into an ambush. I suggest we stay at a safe distance and announce our arrival." Egil's suggestion was accepted by all, so he lifted his hunting horn and blew several long, clear notes.

A brief shout and some rustling noises could just be heard across the water. At least three men had run out of the hut. Two bowmen appeared on a rocky outcrop close to the water. They shouted words in the Niar speech. Fortunately, Weland had spent much of his time at the forge speaking with Geir in his own tongue. He could speak Jutish fluently, and found that the Niars spoke a dialect quite similar to it. The bowmen were asking how many more were in their company.

"Only three adventurers. We request your hospitality." Weland shouted the reply slowly, knowing that his accent would seem strange in these parts. After a few minutes, there was a shrill whistle and six armed figures stepped onto the beach. A Niar voice yelled again.

"We swear by the point of Wotan's spear, we will not harm you if you come ashore with no deception in mind."

Weland looked hard at the warriors and turned to his brothers. "I feel that they have good reason to be cautious, but their quarrel is not with us." The small boat turned, and with a few strong sweeps of the oars, and the scrape of the hull on the pebbly beach, the brothers became the guests of the tall, rough looking warriors.

They were escorted to the hut, which turned out to be somewhat larger than it had seemed from the water. It was, in fact, a mead hall with room at the benches for about fifty warriors. In a sheltered valley within sight of the hall there were many simple dwellings and women and children could be seen moving around. There was a strange air of impermanence, it seemed more like a campsite than a village. The only animals visible were horses, there was no sign of farming, and there were no fishing boats, only four long raiding ships. Several more warriors could be seen returning from hunting carrying a bear and three wild pigs.

The brothers were brought before a man of powerful build wearing armor of exceptional quality. A Thor's Hammer hung from a silver collar at his throat.

"I am Ragnar, The commander here. I offer you our hospitality, but I cannot let you leave until we have achieved our purpose. If you are spies, you would already know who we are. If you really are travellers, it will do no harm to tell you, as our plan will soon succeed.

"I am the son of the previous king, Regin, who was poisoned by my uncle Nidhad's wife when I was a child. Nidhad became king but I remained the heir. My father's most loyal people took me and hid me before the queen could arrange my untimely end. Nidhad's men still seek me.

"I have wide support amongst the people, but they fear the queen. She is a powerful witch and not above making a cruel example of anyone suspected of helping us. She is the real force behind the throne, even the king's astrologer dares not advise the king without consulting her.

"As you can see, I have a force gathered here. Some of the finest warriors in the land have chosen to join me in my bid to rid the land of the tyranny of Nidhad, and his queen who's name is Valrad."

Egil and Slagfid turned to Weland, nominating him as spokesman. He introduced his brothers and himself by name. "We are the sons of King Wada of the Finns. We have come on a quest to prove ourselves worthy of noble status. Wyrd has sent us here. We are trained in swordplay and I am a smith of some note. We will give you whatever help we can."

Ragnar could not hide his surprise at their identity. A grin broadened on his face. "We are cousins then. Your grandsire, your previous king, had a sister who married my grandsire, our king before Regin."

Weland told his brothers excitedly. They had nearly forgotten this piece of family history, not much was heard of that great-aunt but that she was happy with the arrangement, and it had ensured a long peace between their countries.

Ragnar called for mead and a celebration feast for his guests and then returned to business. "You have skill in smithing, do you have some of your work here?"

Weland took his sword by the scabbard so as not to cause alarm. He held the hilt out to Ragnar who drew it slowly. Marvelling at the workmanship, Ragnar stepped back and cleared a space around himself. The balance was perfect in Ragnar's hand as he swung the blade faster and faster until it formed a deadly web of flashing steel around him. He returned the sword to its scabbard. "With blades like these we could not fail. Will you smith for us?"

"Certainly cousin, my hands itch to be back at a forge. I will need tools, and a hut in which to set up the forge."

Ragnar was pleased with this. "There is a deserted hunting lodge in the next valley. It is old but sound, and it has a forge and anvil and a few tools. We can get you anything else you need."

"I would like to get started as soon as possible."

"We will take you there now, if you are not too tired from your journey."

"After sitting in the boat for three days, it would be good to walk in the forest."

Ragnar called some of his men together and made preparations to leave immediately. Without further delay, the small party set off across the valley. As they walked, Ragnar told of the many injustices in the land. He vowed that when he became king, he would earn the respect of the people, like his father King Regin, and their's, King Wada, had done.

Within an hour, the group of warriors stood in the next valley. They found the log cabin in a state of disrepair. Upon closer inspection they saw that it would need only minor repairs to make it quite comfortable. Weland went straight to the forge. The leather of the bellows had rotted away and the anvil and tools were caked in rust, but again a closer look revealed less damage than expected, the forge could be made operational without much work.

Weland was curious, he turned to Ragnar. "What is a smithy doing in the middle of nowhere?"

"There was once a fishing town between here and the water. It was destroyed by pirates who did not think the townsfolk hospitable enough. This is all that remains."

"What was the town called?"

"The town and the surrounding valleys are called Wolfdales. Over that ridge there is a lake, the forest around it is excellent for hunting. Now we must head back to the camp, there are many preparations. The time of our victory will soon be at hand."

At that moment a cloud passed in front of the sun, a small cold gust of wind made them shiver, a raven flew from a nearby tree with a mournful cry. Weland could not feel optimistic about Ragnar's venture.

## Ch 7
# King Nidhad's Hall

Many leagues to the south, King Nidhad sat at the high table in his hall. He was a large man, once known as a fearsome warrior, now barely in his middle years he was becoming fat and weak. He sat, drinking mead from a golden horn, staring morosely at the open doorway.

His astrologer and adviser sat beside him, filling the mead horn, convincing him of the wisdom of the queen's decisions. In contrast to the king, Orm was small and emaciated. His balding head looked more like a fleshless skull. His eyes seemed to bulge in their sunken sockets. Large brown front teeth protruded from under his upper lip, giving him a permanent sneer. With limbs like sticks, he resembled some large insect as he wrung his hands incessantly. He was an exiled Briton and spoke with a noticeable accent.

More than anything, Orm wanted power. With a pretence of knowledge he had impressed the king who appointed him Royal Adviser. The queen, however, had seen through the fraud, but it suited her to keep him at the court. As much as he loved the power he had, he feared her more. So he threatened and dominated those he thought vulnerable to his position, just as the queen did to him.

"Sire, my people have been searching the land for your nephew and his rebels. We have word that they are in the northern forests, in the valleys called Wolfdales. If we send a force of raiding ships led by one of your most loyal jarls, we will crush them. The way will be clear for your sons to rule after you." Orm was anxious to convince the king of the need for action, the queen had the assault planned, but only the jarls could martial a large enough force, and they would only take orders from the king.

"Why don't we just wait for them to come to us. We are well defended here." The king was in an apathetic mood.

"Your nephew may not come here himself. While he lives, the rebels have a leader and a cause. If we act now, we can destroy him and his rebel force."

"Very well, I will talk to Jarl Thorolf tonight."

Orm thanked the king, bowing with obsequious gestures, then ran to find the queen.

"What do you want?" The queen always addressed Orm with an expression of open disgust, as if she were stepping on a crawling insect.

"Your Majesty," Orm grovelled. "I have spoken to the king, he seems ready to take firm action."

"He had better act soon, for your sake." The queen smiled and motioned with her hand for him to leave.

Orm scuttled out, trembling with fear and hate, knowing that the wisdom and magickal power he seemed to have, came only from her. Without her, he was nothing, a charlatan with a lot of useless facts and a handful of tricks.

The queen had felt the presence of Ragnar's force in the north, like a thunder cloud gathering. She had recently seen omens of another force joining it, an individual with powers to match her own. This worried her, she had great plans for her young sons, the spoilt twins, Hrut and Hrolf. When they were old enough, she would set those plans in motion. She would see that the king died conveniently, just as his brother had, and with Ragnar out of the way, her sons would rule. With her help, they would create an empire.

Even her daughter would play a part. Bodhild was still a child, but already she was quite beautiful. She would be a good bargaining piece if they needed an ally or a truce. Her marriage would form a powerful contract with one of the other royal families.

That night, Nidhad spoke to the Commander of the King's Guard, Jarl Thorolf, the king's most trusted jarl. It was decided that the raid should be carried out in secret, thereby avoiding the possibility of interference from jarls sympathetic to the rebels. Three raiding ships would set out tomorrow and three the next day. They would sail out to sea with orders to raid the Finns on the far shore. When out of sight of land, the captains would reveal the new plan, the six ships would group and head northward to Wolfdales.

So it was that six sleek ships sped before an autumn squall, fifty of the best warriors in each. Within three days, they lay at anchor in a deserted bay not far from Wolfdales. Fourty soldiers set off through the forest with scouts going ahead to find the rebel camp. Before nightfall they were in position on a ridge overlooking the camp.

Thorolf and his ships remained in the bay until dawn, and under the cover of the morning mist, rowed silently into the Wolfdales inlet.

The queen lay on her bed with her eyes closed, but she was not asleep. She was viewing the rebel camp, many leagues to the north. Floating high above the scene, she could see the soldiers on the ridge, and the ships in the inlet, and between them the sleeping camp. She could see it all clearly, although to ordinary eyes the whole scene was shrouded in the thick morning mist.

She drifted down and paused for a moment at the doorway of Ragnar's hall. Again she felt the presence, an individual with skill and power, he was near but she could not locate him. She went into the hall.

In Ragnar's dream, he saw the queen standing over him, he could not move. She intoned a curse and laughed.

"You will die today, Ragnar." Her laughter rang with cruel satisfaction, he tried to wake but could not. She vanished suddenly from his dream.

Back in her bed, the queen opened her eyes and stretched. She dressed slowly and went to wake Orm. He was not, however, in his quarters. With a hiss, she went to look for him and found him curled up like a dog in the corner of the king's hall. He had become extremely drunk the night before and had not made it to his bed. She kicked him and he sat up with a startled look. She spoke.

"The trap has been set, the rebels will be crushed today. Tell the king that you have seen it in your dreams."

Orm bowed low, forgetting that he was already on his knees, his forehead hit the slate floor with a sound just like two wooden serving bowls clashing together. This brought a new clarity to the after effects of his excessive consumption of ale and mead. He rolled back into the corner with a groan. The queen ignored him and returned to her chamber.

Some time later, the king entered the hall and dropped himself into his seat. He slumped forward onto the table, a dull ache throbbing in his head. A grunting sound startled him, making his head hurt. The grunting was coming from a pile of rags in the corner. Nidhad picked up a hefty, silver banded drinking horn and hurled it at the source of annoyance. It slammed into Orm's back, knocking the wind out of him. Orm leapt to his feet, gasping for breath and staring wildly around the hall, a small and ineffective looking knife in his hand.

"Don't go killing any giants, Orm. My head couldn't take the noise." Nidhad's fleshy shoulders bounced a little, in time with the rumble of his brief laughter. Orm put the knife away with a sullen look, his own head pounding.

Trying to regain his dignity, Orm put on the act of magician and prophet. "In my dreams I saw portents of the battle at Wolfdales. I saw Ragnar killed and his rebels destroyed." Nidhad regarded Orm with a little more respect. His visions had always been correct, and this fact alone made the loathsome man valuable.

"Your dreams bode well. Thorolf has promised to bring back Ragnar's head. He will return in three days."

Orm smiled and nodded, he felt influential again. He sat beside the king, his skeletal figure expanded slightly with a feeling of self importance.

# Ch 8
## Massacre at Wolfdales

The work at Weland's smithy had progressed well. In three days the forge was operational. The final touch was a boatload of tools and ingots of steel and silver. Everything Weland had asked for and more was somehow supplied through Ragnar's contacts.

The night before the forge was to start producing, Weland and his brothers decided to work late and sleep at the forge to give them an early start in the morning. As the light of dawn began to lift the mist, Weland woke with a feeling of forboding. Once again he had heard the cold laughter of the Niara queen.

He woke the others and strapped on his sword. "We must warn Ragnar, his life is in danger. We don't have much time, it feels bad."

As they ran toward the camp, the mist was lifting, it had snowed during the night and their steps made a soft crunching sound. They ran, blinking in the clean white glare. When they reached the ridge between the valleys, they could hear screams and the ringing of swords. By the time they were half way there, they could see six black raiding ships at the beach and a line of heavily armed soldiers sweeping through the camp, slaughtering all that they found. Screaming people and animals were driven up the far ridge, only to find more soldiers waiting.

The brothers paused in desperation. If they went straight into the battle, they would not have a hope against the tall bearded warriors who outnumbered the surviving rebels three to one. If they stopped, they would have to witness the massacre of their friends.

The decision was taken from them. A small group of lightly armed men and women were running toward them. They were pursued by eight soldiers. The brothers had not yet been seen by any of them. Weland hid behind a bush on one side of the path and his brothers on the other.

As the soldiers passed, three of their number fell, wounds gaping from the unexpected swords. The remaining five turned to do battle. The fleeing rebels, seeing their pursuers stop, turned and joined the melee. The surrounded soldiers formed a circle. They were very large and strong, but the weight of their body armor slowed them just enough.

The fight seemed interminable. Swords whistled and rang, eventually two more soldiers fell. Three of the rebels lay dismembered. Weland was tiring as the three remaining soldiers separated to take the brothers one to one, the rebels had gone.

The soldiers faught extremely well, Weland realized that they must be Nidhad's personal guard. The quality of their arms and armor confirmed this. The tide of the fight turned, the brothers were now in a desperate situation, they could not last much longer. They found themselves being pushed backward down toward the camp. If they were seen, they would be finished.

Echoing up from the waters edge, a long low note sounded from a battle horn. The soldiers paused. Weland's blade ripped up under his foe's chin and into his skull. The other two fled toward the boats. The signal was calling the soldiers back to the beach, they were leaving.

The morning sun shone red through the smoke of burning huts, as the three strode into the wreckage of the camp. Bodies and limbs lay strewn about like dolls broken and discarded. Bright trails and splashes of red told their story, like the brush strokes of some mad artist on the pure white canvas of snow. Ravens gathered in the pines, awaiting their feast once silence had descended.

The hall had collapsed and was still burning fiercely. It was there they found Ragnar's body, not far from the doorway. Its severed arm lay nearby, but the head was nowhere to be seen. Weland knew that the raiders had taken it as proof. It seemed the cause was lost.

With heavy hearts, they returned to the forge, and left the carrion birds to decorate the trees with the entrails of the slain. With the winter snows coming on, they had no time to lose preparing suitable shelter and supplies. The boats had been destroyed in the raid and they did not have the skill to build a seaworthy craft. They had seen no sign of the few survivors of the raid. They deduced that the last of the rebels had set off on foot to the nearest village, but the forest was too vast and unfamiliar for the brothers to try to find it.

In the next two weeks, three new cabins were built within sight of the smithy. After spending so much time living in the same boat, room, or tent, it was a welcome change to have their own comfortable dwellings. By the time they had settled in and produced all of the tools they would need to survive the winter, the snow was falling steadily. While Weland created sharp steel heads for arrows and spears, the others made the shafts and bows. They also made snowshoes, they now floundered waist deep without them.

Each morning, they would set off into the forest to collect storable foods and hunt deer, bear, and wild pig. In the afternoon, they would start smoking the meat and store the food in a small shed in which everything stayed frozen.

# Ch9
# The Valkyries

The brothers had not returned to the rebel camp since the day of the battle. They would rather have burned the corpses, but to collect all of the bodies and enough wood to burn them on would have taken days and put their own survival at risk. However, the howling of large numbers of wolves at night left them in no doubt that the disposal of corpses was being attended to.

One misty morning, the three set off on their snow shoes toward the lake where Ragnar had said there was good hunting. He had called it Wolf Lake and they certainly saw many wolf tracks as they ran through the forest into its valley. Despite the number of wolves inhabiting Wolfdales, tracks of more edible animals were plentiful.

They spotted the tracks of a large deer, on it fresh droppings still steamed in the cold air. Running with a bouncing gait, they soon came within sight of their prey then separated to stalk from different directions.

The deer became restless as it caught their scent, but Egil was within range with his bow. Before the animal could dart away, he loosed a well aimed arrow at its heart. Just as the arrow left the bow, Slagfid swore. He had fallen through the snow into a small stream hidden below. He was quick enough to lift his feet out of the freezing water before his boots became soaked, but the startled deer turned and the arrow plunged into its flank.

Egil cursed, the deer would not live long, but they may have to chase it for some distance before it dropped. It took off up the valley toward the lake with three hunters running in pursuit. They soon lost sight of it through the trees and had to follow the tracks and drops of fresh blood in the snow, its color reminding them of the massacre at the rebel camp.

At last they saw the blue water through the trees, and on the lake's shore stood the deer. It staggered and turned toward them, then coughed and fell to the ground. As they approached the lake, they noticed that the snow thinned and stopped well before the waters edge. A strange mist rose from its surface, the lake itself was quite small.

Just as they were sobering from the wonder of this unearthly place, they were struck dumb by the sight of three young women swimming out of the mist.

"Come swimming, young hunters." They teased. "Are you afraid of water." The women had seen the brothers approaching and had concealed themselves in the misty waters.

Egil was suspicious and whispered. "I have heard of such spirits, they will lure us into the water where we will freeze to death or drown."

Speaking low, Weland replied. "These are not spirits, but I sense their power. We should not offend them. Take off your clothes." Then he addressed the women. "We would be delighted to join you, fair maidens." He threw off his garments and without hesitation, jumped into the water. Bracing himself against the expected cold, he was surprised that the water was actually warm. With a stern glance from Weland, the other two followed.

The brothers introduced themselves but the women merely smiled and splashed them. Weland addressed them again politely. "Why do you travel so far from your homelands in the south." He had guessed from their strange accents and the fact that one of them was very small and dark of hair.

Hearing this, the smallest spoke. "I am Olrun from the court of King Kiarval of Valland."

"I am Hlathgud and this is my sister Hervor, we are from the court of King Hlothver of the Franks. Wyrd has sent us here, we could not refuse."

At this, they swam to another part of the lake and the brothers followed. The women stepped out of the water, unconcerned by their nakedness, and started to dry themselves. Weland saw that they each had a cape of swan feathers beside her clothes. He knew then that these were valkyries.

The brothers waded out of the lake and sat beside the valkyries. They talked of their travels and before long they had paired off, Egil with Olrun, Slagfid with Hlathgud, and Weland with Hervor. For a long time they smiled and played together, until each brother found himself in an embrace in which he lost himself in ecstasy.

"Come back to our cabins, they are more comfortable than your small tent." Weland was infatuated, so were his brothers.

"Our work is finished here, but we can stay with you at least for the winter." Hervor's smile was open and affectionate. Weland knew that these women were powerful and could not be kept against their will. He felt blessed that they would stay even for a while.

During the winter months, isolated from the world by the deepening snow, the brothers grew to love their remarkable partners more with each day. Their strength and wisdom, far beyond their years, contrasted with a childlike, carefree innocence. An innocence without ignorance, which accepted life as it was. Free of desires, they partook of nature's gifts with joy.

Hervor taught Weland a little about the work of the valkyrie. The warrior-preistess would follow those lines of wyrd which culminated in a knot of battle. They would sit not far from the battle field to watch the start of combat, then enter a trance in which they would fly above the fight and assist the dead to find the correct direction for their particular journey.

The valkyries practiced a powerful system of magic which utilised sexual energy, they called it "seidh" and it was first taught by the goddess Freya. Hervor introduced Weland to the basic theory and practice, and this gave them much to do during the long hours of darkness in the months when the sun barely left the horizon, illuminating only the tops of the hills for a few hours a day.

His perception of the Wyrd grew to the point that he was beginning to see the subtler connections between any two events, and the multitude of possibilities branching from each decision. Although he had long been proficient in divination and the casting of spells, he was now starting to perceive how the lines of wyrd could be influenced or read directly, thus making it possible to predict or influence events. He saw that his every action sent out strands of connection which became a complex web of interaction with intersecting strands forming multi-dimensional runes which changed their shape and meaning as his perspective changed. The runes which the god Wotan had brought back from the well of the unmanifest were two dimensional projections of the intersections which typified various kinds of interaction. The 24 runes given to humankind reflected the human perspective of these interactions, the other orders of being each had its own unique set of runes.

In the spring, when the thick blanket of snow had receded to the higher slopes, the brothers went further afield to hunt and explore the surrounding country, while the women enjoyed a rest from their travelling. It was on one of their expeditions that they came across an old man setting snares. It was quite some distance from Wolfdales and this was the first sign of other humans they had seen since the massacre. They stopped to share some food and conversation with the old man.

They learned that he was from a village upstream from Wolf inlet, and that there were more such villages all along that river. Because the river was so fast flowing above the inlet, the towns were safe from pirate raids.

"Where the river widens out into Wolf inlet, and the water slows, there is Wolfdales. There was once a town there too, but it was too vulnerable to raids. Even before that, the place was considered unlucky. I have heard that there are ancient graves in one of the valleys, filled with gold, but cursed. Avoid the place if you can." With that, the old man stood up and shook their hands. "I must be off now, if I'm going to be home before dark."

They watched him until he was out of sight and hurried back to their own homes. As they walked, they talked about the gold and its likely location. Weland wondered if the Wolfdales villagers had violated the graves, perhaps they were the source of Ragnar's wealth, and a cause of his death.

The weather warmed and the days became long and joyful. Their first summer was peaceful and abundant. Weland spent much of his time honing his skills at the forge, working the steel and silver to create exquisite daggers and brooches. These he sold in the villages for the little gold they could muster. He wanted to make a golden arm ring for Hervor but he would not have enough gold for quite some time.

While not at the forge, when hunting or walking through the forest, he would practice seeing the wyrd of weather. He soon became quite skilled in predicting and even influencing it. This earned him the name Weland the Weather-Wise amongst his friends in the village. When they discovered that he had been living in Wolfdales apparently unscathed, they added "elf-friend" and even "elf-leader" to his name. It was not long before people from the village, and even from villages up river, would come to consult him for guidance and healing.

As his reputation grew, it was only a matter of time before the queen heard of his skill in magic and metals. It now became clear to her that he was the force she had long felt residing in Wolfdales. Now knowing his name, she could see him and the others on her nightly travels, and set about weaving a plan to bring him under her control. He would be a valuable tool to use in her ambitious schemes.

Just as Valrad had become aware of Weland, he too became aware of her more direct attention. While his dreams of her laughter had been a portent, now she came to weave his wyrd with her own. Although Weland and the Valkyries set up a powerful magical barrier, he knew that his wyrd was already entwined with Valrad's. Sooner or later, he would have to face her and work through the events which would unravel the tangled strands which bound them together.

# Ch 10
# The Curse

For seven years all went well at Wolfdales. There was always an abundance of food, and anything they could not find or make could be bought at the nearest village with Weland's handwork.

As the weather became cooler with the shortening days of late summer, Egil and Slagfid decided to investigate the valley on the other side of the rebel camp. They had not been back to the camp since the massacre and went a little out of their way to skirt around it. They came close enough, however, to see the pile of charred logs where the hall had been, and everywhere the litter of human bones, broken and scattered by scavengers.

Making their way up the far ridge, they were glad to leave the unfortunate valley behind. At the top of the ridge, they found more bones where the soldiers had cut off the retreat, and more here and there down the other side.

They stopped half way down to survey a narrow valley with steep wooded sides and many rocky outcrops showing through the trees. They could hear a small stream coursing along its rock strewn bed some distance below. To the north, the marshy mouth of the stream could be seen emptying into the tranquil waters of Wolf inlet. To the south, the stream marked the bottom of the valley, which ran in an almost straight line half a league toward a squat and rounded mountain, there to burrow between two of its spurs. Something about the mountain intrigued them, and with unspoken agreement Egil and Slagfid made their way southward.

It was not long before they entered into the perpetual shadow of the north side of the mountain. Standing in the cleft between the spurs, they looked back out along the deep, narrow valley, sunlit except for the very southern end in which they stood. It was cool and damp, mosses covered the rocks and trees. Egil turned toward the mountain.

"The stream seems to start not far up from here. By the amount of water in it so close to its source, and the fact that it hasn't rained for three days, it must be fed by a spring."

"Let's have a look." Slagfid was already striding ahead as he spoke.

The air was musty with the smell of decomposing wood and leaves. Boulders and scattered vegetation made it difficult to see very far ahead and they were soon climbing quite steeply. They followed the course of the stream which they could hear running beneath and between the tumbled rocks.

They came at last to a wide shelf upon which grew a grove of tall pines. Beyond the trees, the mountain continued its ascent with a sheer cliff face. There was no way up, but neither was there any sign of water coming down. The rock face was dry, yet the small stream flowed as strongly here as it had in the valley. It issued mysteriously from a clump of bushes at the base of the cliff.

As they approached the bushes, it seemed that the rock was much darker behind the foliage than the grey of the cliff. It was only when they parted the bushes that they saw the cave from which the stream was given birth. Although they both felt a strange urge to investigate further, Egil and Slagfid had always kept at a prudent distance from caves, one never knew what dangerous beasts or demons lurked within.

As they turned to leave, something caught Egil's eye. There was a metallic glint at the base of one of the bushes. He strode forward and picked up a gold brooch. Stories of dragons' hoards and ancient kings ran through their minds. Drawing their swords, they went into the cave's cool darkness.

Standing near the cave mouth, blinking and peering as their eyes adjusted to the gloom, the brothers found that the cavern was much larger than they had expected. The stream bubbled out of an unseen fissure somewhere further into the mountain, dividing the wide cave floor in two with a narrow channel. Gradually more features became visible.

The back of the cave still receded into blackness with no sign of narrowing, but off to each side, smaller passages could now be discerned. Slagfid peered into one of these and hissed to Egil.

"I can't see a thing in there, we need some light. I will make a fire just outside if you can find something to use as a torch."

While Slagfid lit the fire with flint and tinder, Egil found some pine cones and stuck them onto sharpened sticks. With their new torches, they hurried back into the cave. It was now clear that they were in a tunnel which ran straight back into the mountain beyond the torch light, with passages leading off to each side at regular intervals. The first few passages were just empty chambers, but not too far in they found one which glittered with gold and jewels. Its state of disorder suggested that it had been disturbed and partially looted.

"This is probably a cursed tomb." Egil's voice seemed to boom through the mountain and he reduced it to a whisper. "We should bring Weland here."

But Slagfid's eyes shone with treasure-lust. "I'll just take a few little things for him to see." So they filled their hunting bags with as much as they could carry, avoiding as much as possible the remains of some long dead warrior, and set off home.

Weland had been feeling uneasy all day. When his hammer smote upon the anvil, it seemed to ring with the bitter triumph of Valrad's laughter. Indeed she was at that time on Saevarstead island, not far from Nidhad's hall, weaving her wyrd with his, a net with which to ensnare him. Orm carried a large goat horn full of a foul smelling potion. Standing within a circle of white quartz stones, she turned her face to the north, eyes shining with malice, and pointed an ornate dagger toward Wolfdales.

"Weland smith, strands of wyrd I wind about thee.
Far sight and fear, foe to thee I may be.
Soon on Saevarstead, slave to me thou shalt be."

As if in answer, a long rumble of thunder rolled in the distance behind her. She turned to see a dark storm front to the south. Orm fell to his knees trembling, a drop of dark liquid spilled onto his hand. Valrad glared at him.

"Your wyrd is bound with his, fool. Get up!" She took the horn from him and walked slowly around the circle, stopping at each of the four quarters. As she held the horn aloft, she intoned a different combination of vowels for each quarter. Returning to the centre, she tipped the liquid slowly onto the ground.

"Blood for blood, life for life.
Into the soil of Saevarstead.
Imprisoned you shall be."

When they had finished, they hurried back to the boat. Orm rowed as fast as his scrawny arms could manage and they reached the shore near Nidhad's hall just as the storm broke.

Nor was that the only storm about to break. Valrad had managed to persuade Nidhad and the Jarl of the Southern Mark that some of the farmlands of the Svears to the south should be paying tribute to the Niars. This land had been settled by the Svears generations ago but did originally belong to the Niars. For the first time, the Niars were not on friendly terms with their southern neighbors. Nidhad was troubled by this, but Valrad's silver tongue quickly convinced him that the claim was just. After some months of heated negotiations, the jarls were preparing for war.

Away to the north in Wolfdales, Weland heard the rumble of the approaching tempest. He felt suddenly tired, and a chill on his spine made him shiver, despite the roaring heat of the forge. As the sky darkened with cloud, a heavy despair crept over him, he began to worry about his brothers. Dropping his hammer, he strode over to his cabin to find Hervor also in a heavy mood. He cast a glance through the open door behind him.

"Something is wrong, it feels as though happiness has left this valley. I fear for my brothers."

Hervor closed her eyes for a moment and spoke with a voice devoid of her usual light heartedness. "Your brothers will return, but we valkyries may soon have to leave. Battle is brewing in the south and we are feeling restless. The day is approaching when we will wear our swan feather cloaks again." She seemed distant, as if a part of her was already on its way south. Realising that argument would be useless, Weland turned and walked slowly back toward the smithy.

A shout stopped him at its door. He spun around to see his brothers running down the steep hillside at a dangerous pace. He started to reach for the sword which hung just inside the door, looking for his brothers' persuers on the ridge, until he saw the grins on their faces and heard what they were shouting.

"Gold! A dragon's hoard of gold and jewels."

They burst into the smithy, dragging Weland with them, and emptied their hunting bags onto the work bench. Weland gasped at the sight.

"Where did you find this?" He felt dizzy, the treasure seemed to radiate a feeling of malice. "It must be cleansed, but I fear the worst is already upon us." Weland told them of his feeling of forboding and of the impending war in the south which Hervor had forseen. He chose, however, not to disclose that this could mean the departure of the valkyries.

# Ch 11
# The Prisoner

For the next month, the brothers busied themselves with a rigorous cleansing ritual in an effort to avert some of the misfortune about to descend upon them. Weland constructed a circle of stones and dug a deep pit in the center. He instructed his brothers to bury the treasure in it and light a fire on top. Without food, drink, or sleep each took his turn tending to the fire. Weland carved many runes on each log and in the silent hours before dawn it seemed that the wood squealed and hissed with tiny voices as it burned.

With the extra work involved in their ritual, the brothers hardly noticed that the valkyries were busy with their own preparations. Each day they would stride off into the forest shortly after dawn, and each day they took longer to return. When asked about it they replied that they had their own purification rites to observe.

One evening, with the month long vigil almost over, Egil returned to his hut to break his fast after his turn at the fire. The hut was dark and cold. He went to Slagfid's hut. It too was empty, Slagfid had gone straight to the fire after hunting to take his turn.

When Egil entered Weland's hut he saw the smith staring into the embers of his small fire, motionless. "Weland, it is getting late. Perhaps we should search for the women."

"Egil, we have heard rumours of war brewing in the south. These women are valkyries. We cannot know what oath binds them but they are drawn to the battle, they may not return."

For some time Egil gaped dumbly at Weland then turned and ran to Slagfid at the fire. They returned minutes later. "We are going to join them. We have some dried fish and some gold from beneath the fire."

"You may have done more harm than you know, but I wish you well. Keep these stones with the gold, they should help counter any ill effects. I will stay here and do what I can to bring them back."

He handed them some small stones which looked like icicles and they packed them with the gold without question. They clasped hands briefly and Weland found himself suddenly alone, a great tiredness driving him inexorably toward oblivion.

It was mid afternoon before he woke and his eyes ached in the glare of daylight, despite the unbroken blanket of gray cloud above. He made his way slowly to the treasure pit, the embers of the fire were now cold but scattered amongst them gold and jewels glittered in mockery of the dead flames. He placed the scattered pieces in the leather bag in which they had been buried and set off toward the smithy.

Weland emptied the heavy bag on his work bench and sorted the items into piles according to their nature. Last of all, he gathered the large number of gold arm rings and threaded them onto a piece of rope and hung them on a hook on the wall. He sat for a while on his anvil and gazed at them.

After a moment or an eternity, he could not tell, the small black man appeared before him. Weland spoke with a dreamy voice.

"It has been long since I saw you, what is your name?"

"It has been but the blink of a fish's eye, call me Svartalf."

"You are a guardian of the dark places in the earth and the glittering gold and jewels therein."

"Gold glitters not in my realm, the brightest amethyst is as black as soot."

"What value is treasure in the dark?"

"What value is light if it blinds you? Your smiths powers were forged in darkness, just as the gold under the mountains."

"Have I neglected my progress?"

"You have become stronger than ever, but your life here would have become lazy and stagnant before too long. Your greatest ordeal awaits you."

"Where is my weakness, why do I fear?"

"Seek not to see differences when all things are the same in the end. Do what you must, but make it always a work of art."

"Where do I start?"

"Fashion a gold arm ring for your love and bind it with spells of lust."

"Will it bring her back?"

"No, but it will bring you back. Do not let hope blind you."

With a mocking cackle, the black elf vanished leaving Weland suddenly aware of his hunger. He realised that he had not eaten for almost a full day. Daylight was fading as he consumed most of the remaining provisions. He soon fell, once again, into a long and dreamless slumber.

Waking early, with the golden light of dawn staining the scattered clouds with the color of the finest mead, Weland went straight to the forge to start work on the ring. After some thought, he decided that the design should be plain but perfect. He melted down some of the damaged rings and removed the dross. Every movement became an invocation to Freya. By nightfall he was pleased with the result.

Hanging the new ring on the rope, Weland returned to his hut to finish the last of the food and retired early, for tomorrow he would have to go hunting. The first snow of autumn was falling and he risked starvation if he did not stock up before winter.

In the pre-dawn darkness the smith took his bow and six straight shafts and strode across the thin white crust of new snow into the fastness of the ancient forest. It was midday before he found tracks, a half grown bear, which he followed until mid afternoon. With two carefully aimed shots he dispatched the animal and gutted it where it fell. He slung the carcass across his shoulders and trudged home.

As he approached the huts, he thought he saw faint footprints in the snow. Although the light was failing and fresh snow had begun to fall, he saw that the prints were smaller than his own. Dropping the bear meat outside the smithy door, he entered and kindled a small fire in the forge, by its light he could see that nothing had been disturbed. He took the loop of rope from the wall upon which hung the numerous rings of gold and his heart stopped, the plainest of them was missing.

"It must be her." Weland's mind held only one thought.

He hurried back to his hut with a piece of meat to cook, and when he had eaten, he sat awaiting his beloved. Tiredness, however, overcame him, and he did not hear the soft crunch of footsteps on the white carpet outside. A loud crash made him leap to his feet, soldiers in steel helmets had broken his door down and others had burst in through the roof. As he reached for his sword, a sickening blow to his head thrust him into oblivion.

While Weland had been hunting, a Niar raiding ship had moored in Wolfdales inlet, three boys were sent out as scouts, one of whom found the smithy and took the ring as evidence thinking that the plainest ring would be the least likely to be missed. The captain was a minor jarl with great ambitions, he agreed to capture Weland for the Queen in return for her help. Queen Valrad's influence had grown steadily over the years, and so had her reputation for witchcraft. Many who felt that they were not achieving enough power in the King's service went to her to bargain for a better deal. Thus she gained a hold over many whose ambition made them willing to act for her behind the King's back.

When Weland woke he found himself bound and fettered, it was mid morning, he was at sea, and his head ached. He was given food and when he sat up he could see land about a league to the right. He knew then that he was bound for Nidhad's hall.

# Ch 12
## Saebarstead

Two days later, as the sun set behind distant white mountains, the raiding ship turned its prow toward the failing light and a sheltered bay in which Weland could soon see many similar craft at anchor.

The ship beached near some large wooden buildings and a dozen soldiers jumped into the shallow water dragging Weland with them. Once inside the main hall they threw him down upon his knees, before him stood a pale and skeletal apparition. It spoke in a sneering, arrogant tone.

"I am Orm, the King's counsellor. Your life is in my hands, you would do well to co-operate."

"I am Weland and I hold the strands of your wyrd. You will die ere my work is done here."

Orm's face turned even whiter, then bright crimson as it twisted in rage. He drew a slim dagger but before he could lift it to strike, Nidhad entered the hall.

"So we have a rebel spy from Wolfdales. I thought we cleaned out that rat hole. Living on the riches that my ungrateful nephew stole from me. Why have you brought him here? You should have killed him on the spot, like the rest of those vermin."

Valrad was now standing behind the King and spoke softly. "This is Weland, he has great skill as a smith. We should put him to work for us."

The King turned slowly and shrugged. "Very well, I will have a smithy set up. I could do with some new treasures. You can work to replace some of the valuables you obviously stole from me. My men found quite a hoard in Wolfdales."

Weland sneered in contempt. "I have seen nothing in this land that compares to the treasures in the house where I was born."

By this time the whole royal family had wandered in to see what was going on. Nidhad's sons stood in a corner staring. His daughter Bodhild, beautiful and vain, stood beside him and Weland saw Hervor's gold ring on her arm. From Nidhad's belt hung Weland's sword. Valrad spoke low once more.

"Look at his eyes, he would slay us all if he could. We should cripple him and put him on Saevarstead island to work for us."

Nidhad agreed and Weland was taken to the soldiers huts. They bound him to a post and severed the hamstrings of his right leg then sealed the wound with a hot iron. When they took him down, they tied his ankle to his belt so that when the wound healed he would not be able to straighten his leg.

As he lay in fever for the next month, he drifted in his mind so that it became hard to tell where the dreams ended and the waking nightmare began. Sometimes he would see the great striped cat, and it would carry him on its back. They would race though the forest and hunt the deer, with its claws like sickles and teeth like long curved daggers. They would feast together on the raw meat and Weland felt stronger, free and wild.

Sometimes he saw his teacher, Geir, and the nomad healer, Kveld, standing together watching and smiling. Often he saw Svartalf who seemed to speak in riddles. Weland always felt that he had learned something from the riddles but he was never sure exactly what. One night, when Weland was over the worst and making a rapid recovery, Svartalf appeared.

"Svartalf, is this the ordeal of which you spoke?"
"The ordeal has only just begun."
"How shall I regain my strength?"
"Practice your craft."
"What comes next?"
"The art of revenge."
"Where do I start?"
"You must always keep a promise, go to Orm and Kill him."
"But I cannot walk."
"You need legs no longer, follow me."

Weland felt himself float up through the roof of the hut and over to the main hall. Passing through a wall, he found himself in the sleeping quarters at the back, hovering over the snoring body of Orm. The bundle of bones stirred and turned onto its back. Slowly Orm's eyes opened and grew steadily wider until they seemed to bulge from their sockets. Realizing that he had no weapon, the smith drew a bindrune in the air which hung glowing above the hapless creature. Weland took the rune and plunged it into Orm's chest.

A distant scream brought Weland suddenly back to his hut, he could hear soldiers running toward the hall. After some shouting and a false alarm signal on a horn, the soldiers could be heard returning to their huts. As they approached, Weland heard them talking.

"It was just that clown Orm having a nightmare. He says the prisoner was trying to kill him."

"The prisoner won't be going anywhere for a while on that leg."

"We'd better check anyway......I can see him. I'm going back to bed."

There was much muttering amongst the soldiers the next day and Weland overheard that Orm was ill in bed. The soldiers did not have much sympathy for him. Later that afternoon Valrad came to the smith's hut.

"Fine aid you gave to Orm last night, to help him sleep perhaps? No matter, he has served his purpose. I will not be such an easy target. You are to go now to Saevarstead, the island just here in the bay, a smithy has been set up for you. You are to commence immediately, jewels and metals have been left there as well as enough provisions for a month. We will bring supplies and collect your works every month. If you don't work, you won't eat. There is no escape."

Weland merely grinned at her, which so disturbed her that she turned and strode away without another word. The guards dragged him to a small boat and rowed him to the island where they sat him at the forge and left.

The smithy was comfortable and well tooled, at the back was a bed, a trunk, and a couple of stools. Winter had now begun and the snow on the ground was now permanent. With every blow of hammer on anvil, Weland felt stronger. Day and night he produced exquisite works, and when the first month had passed, Nidhad himself came to see them and was well pleased.

"You have done well, smith. My campaign in the south was short and decisive. The Svears on my land are now paying tribute. With that and your contribution we will be the wealthiest kingdom in the region."

Weland smiled, he was in no hurry and his best pieces were in the locked trunk in the corner. Each month Nidhad returned and each month he was more impressed with the treasures.

# Ch 13
# Revenge

When in late spring the snow had retreated to the nearby mountains, Nidhad came to Saevarstead with his sons who were now quite large and had wispy hairs trailing from their chins and pimply faces. They had their father's propensity for gaining weight if under exercized, and were obviously enjoying a pampered life. As usual, the King was pleased with Weland's work and left the smithy carrying many fine objects. The boys, however, were curious and tarried by the forge until their father had set off toward the boat. When the King was out of hearing, they turned haughtily toward Weland.

"Show us what is in the trunk, smith."

Weland opened it for them and they gasped at the sight of treasures which seemed to becon them to touch. The wiley smith saw the gold lust in their eyes. He gave each a jeweled cloak pin, then spoke low in a conspiratorial manner.

"This will help you start your own hoards. If you come here again secretly, we will look for pieces more suitable for future kings. Tell no-one lest their rumours bring the King's annoyance upon you."

Nidhad had reached the boat by now and was calling. The boys ran down to it laughing excitedly about their secret.

About two weeks later Weland woke as usual, well before dawn. He was just starting to pump the large bellows when the boys walked in. They had taken a small rowing boat and set out unseen in the pre-dawn mist and darkness.

"Open the chest, smith. We are here to claim our treasure."

"Certainly, my princes, you have surely earned your share of riches, and your place in history which this visit shall ensure."

Once more the trunk was opened and the boys' eyes opened with it. They knelt before the glittering hoard and picked out objects the like of which they had never before seen. The priceless works held them in such thrall that they hardly noticed when Weland knelt down between them and placed his sinewy arms upon their shoulders.

"Our little secret." Weland laughed, as he slid an arm around each neck as if to hug them closer to him. The hug, however did not relent. The smiths arms became bands of steel around each neck. Weland could feel them struggle uselessly as he slowly increased the force of his hold. For all their size, the pampered muscles of the twins could make no impression against thews hardened by years of dedicated work. With a heave of the smith's chest, he heard and felt a loud cracking from the hapless necks. He relaxed letting the bodies fall limply from under each arm.

He reached for a recently forged sword and hewed off the heads with easy strokes, then threw their bodies into the pit which formed the air chamber of the bellows. He took the dripping heads outside and worked carefully with a smalll wood saw to cut off the top of the skulls, just above the eyebrows. He then extracted the teeth with his smallest tongs. The remains he smashed carefully into small fragments with a hammer and left for the ravens.

Weland became aware of the growing light of dawn and made his way to the beach while the morning mist still gave cover. He rowed the boys' small boat to the other side of the island and hobbled back to the smithy. He then set about making the finest of his creations yet.

He carved the teeth and set them in gold constructing brooches of unsurpassed beauty. The skulls he lined with silver inside and the outer surfaces he carved and inlaid with gold and precious stones, creating a pair of drinking bowls of unequalled exquisiteness.

When the King arrived looking somewhat worried, Weland showed him the new creations. Nidhad's spirits were lifted instantly.

"Never have I seen the like of these in any court or any hoard brought from afar." Then his marvelling countenance turned grave once more.

"What troubles you my lord?"

"Orm has died of a lingering illness, and my sons have gone off on some adventure. It has been a week since they were last seen. Perhaps you can work some of your magic. It is said that you are a friend of elves."

"Of course Sire. Fill these cups with the finest mead and toast nightly to the return of the princes. You shall kiss their brows ere you next stand on Saevarstead."

Nidhad turned toward the door and absently muttered his thanks to the smith and returned to his hall, and it was indeed as Weland had said, as Nidhad and his queen drank from the skulls of their sons.

Weland once more turned his thoughts toward the King's hall, seeking his next prey. Bodhild was now a beautiful young woman. His next move required timing. From beneath his bed he took a leather pouch containing twenty-four small peices of wood, on each of which was carved a different rune. Concentrating his mind with his intent, he summoned the power of the runes and felt the hair bristle on his neck as an involuntary shiver ran down his back. The power of the runes is the power of Wotan, a god of wisdom and magick, but also of war and revenge. In the scattered staves which fell from the pouch, Weland's wyrd became once again clear. He would do what he must.

The smith held an image in his mind, the ring he had made and charged for Hervor. He set about constructing a copy of the ring and poured forth his lust into it and into the original. To Bodhild the ring started to feel warm and her thoughts went often to the mysterious prisoner of Saevarstead. The effect was subtle at first, but Bodhild became increasingly distracted as the days passed. After a week, the ring seemed to writhe and wake her in the night, she would feel sudden urges, passionate and lustful. These moods were always strongest after the sun had set.

One such evening she found herself taking pleasure in the thought of abandoning herself to the pure carnality of her urges. Coming suddenly to an awareness that the ring had become uncomfortably warm, she tried to remove it from her arm. It seemed to fight her. As she pulled at it in panic, it broke, although she could not have had the strength to break it herself.

Desolate about the broken ring, she decided to go that night to Weland to have it fixed. Arriving before midnight, she entered the smithy shivering from the cold night air.

"I have come here secretly because I do not want to arouse my father's suspicion or anger. I do not know how the ring broke but I must have it fixed."

"I can repair it within the hour and it will look better than ever."

Weland took out a cask of mead which Nidhad had given him as a reward for his work and persuaded her to have a drink to fortify herself against the cold. She was soon very tipsy and the passions she had felt became overpowering. She threw off her clothes and stretched out on his bed, the warmth of the forge fuelling her lust. Finding his crippled leg no impediment, Weland released himself into the storm of carnal instinct and became mighty drinking the awesome power of nature's purest expression. In deep satisfaction, Bodhild soon drifted into a peaceful slumber.

Knowing that his ordeal was now completed, Weland took some provisions and his finest works in a leather bag and hobbled away to the boat he had hidden on the other side of the island. He pointed the prow to the east, pushed off, and started rowing. When a safe distance out to sea, he lay down to await the dawn.

Not long before sunrise, Bodhild woke with a start. She saw Weland standing near the forge and smiled, until she remembered her nakedness. She remembered what she had done and although she did not regret it, she feared it. She heard Weland laugh, then she saw him float up to the roof. In terror she grabbed her clothes and ran screaming to her boat. She returned to her bed before she was missed and told no-one of her visit.

After four days on the sea and a day following the coast of his homeland, Weland arrived at his father's hall. Egil and Slagfid were already there, having given up on their search when its futility became plain. A great feast was held to welcome him and he told the tale of his capture, his hamstringing, the months on Saevarstead, and his revenge. Afterward he went to speak to Geir alone. There was one more thing to be done.

Weland arranged to meet Geir at their hunting lodge in the forest the next night. Geir brought a drum which Kveld had made for him, a skin stretched over a hoop of wood. Weland lay still on the bed while Geir started to beat steadily on the drum.

Slowly, Weland felt himself rising, then suddenly becoming a black falcon circling above the hall of King Nidhad. He perched in a tall tree in front of the hall and regained human form. He called loudly for Nidhad who stumbled from the hall somewhat drunk. Nidhad's visit to Saevarstead was not due for another couple of days, thus Weland's absence had not been discovered.

Too drunk to wonder how, or why, a crippled man would swim across half a mile of freezing water and climb so tall a tree, Nidhad yelled up at him.

"Get back to your island, smith. I'm in no mood for any pranks. Where are my sons, they have still not returned as you said they would."

"First you must swear that any grandchild of thine or its mother, though it live in your hall, you shall keep safe from all harm. Swear by the bulwark of your ship and your sword's point and the tip of Wotan's spear."

"Of course I swear."

"Very well! You have nightly kissed your sons' brows with each toast of their return. The smith has thrown their bodies in the bellows pit and fashioned your precious cups from their skulls. With their teeth he made brooches for Bodhild and Valrad."

Valrad had just appeared and shrieked a wordless curse at him. She motioned the bowmen to fire but their arrows clattered uselessly around him.

"Nor is that all the news I have tonight. Bodhild is with child, your only heir shall be mine also."

Laughing he became a black falcon and flew into the east.

The drumming slowed as he opened his eyes.

"It is done."

"So I see."

They drank mead and talked of the many things that had happened since Weland's departure. Geir smiled and seemed to stare into a great distance.

"I have seen your works. The student is now a Master. I have never seen the equal of your craft, there is little more I can teach you, my work here is finished. The King will no longer need my arts, and my good wife died last year. My life here has been good but I have more to learn and I must continue my journey."

"Will you return to the Jutish lands?"

"There is nothing there for me. I will go north and stay with my friend Kveld, he is a great healer and knows the tree which joins the realms. Farewell."

With that they clasped hands and understood each others minds. Geir strode out of the cabin toward his own hut, he and some of his belongings were gone the next day. He was never again seen in those parts.

The years went well for Weland and his skill in metals became still greater. His fame spread far and all of the Kings in the region went to great lengths to acquire his work. When his father died, he became king and ruled wisely and was well loved just as Wada had been.

When Nidhad died, his only heir was Bodhild's son Widia. When Weland visited King Widia they soon became great friends. Widia was glad to get to know his father of whom he had heard only legends. Weland helped him to regain the friendship of the Svears and achieve lasting peace and prosperity in the region.

When Weland was quite old he gave the kingship to Egil and went north in a small boat and was never seen again. His works, however, became legend, and the story of his skill and the magical weapons and rings he created has been told throughout the countries north of the Rhine for centuries. Most often told is the story of his revenge.

# Exit the Skald

When Unfrith the skald had finished, not a warrior stirred. They sat at the benches staring in wonder at the poet who had brought the well known story to life so vividly.

Without a further word, Unfrith strode toward the door and into the snow and night's darkness. It was only after the sound of his footprints had vanished that King Eystein and his Jarls realized as one that the skald had possessed only one eye, and the staff on which he had been leaning was really a great spear. Although the fire in the central trench was still quite warm, they all shivered when the true identity of their guest dawned upon them.

# Further Reading

This is a short list of books which are particularly recommended. For broader book lists covering the Northern traditions see the bibliographies of the following books and the Asatru links listed on our web site.

Our Troth, Kveldulf Gundarsson, Booksurge, 2006

The Rune Primer, S. Plowright, Lulu, 2006

Lords of Battle, Stephen Evans, Boydell Press, 1997

The Viking Art of War, Paddy Griffith, Greenhill Books, 1995

Anglo-Saxon Military Institutions on the Eve of the Norman Conquest, C. Warren Hollister, Oxford University Press, 1962

The Sword in Anglo-Saxon England, H. R. Ellis Davidson, Boydell Press, 1962

Germania, Tacitus, Penguin Classics, 1970

Egil's Saga, Transl. Pálsson & Edwards, Penguin Classics, 1976

The Saga of the Volsungs, Transl. J. Byock, University of California Press, 1990

True Hearth, James Chisholm, Runa Raven Press, 1993

The Power of Internal Martial Arts, B. Frantzis, North Atlantic Books, 1998

# Useful contacts for those on the path

## Useful Web Addresses

### Rune-Net

http://www.mackaos.com.au/Rune-Net

Rune-Net home page. We will keep a link on this page for True Helm supplements & info.

For Rune-Net members-only site, e-mail me: sweyn@au.mensa.org

### STAV

http://www.stavinternational.org

### New Northvegr

http://www.northvegr.org

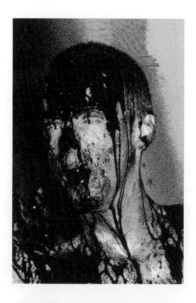

# Mark Morte
Immersing himself in his medium

Well known Sydney artist and musician, Morte always has many projects happening. His works include paintings, murals, underground comic illustration, performance art, and storyboards for film and TV.

On the underground music scene he is known for his performances in the bands Navigating Man's Ruin, Beastianity, and as a past vocalist and lyricist in Naxzul. He has been described as the archetypal Granny Shocker.

Sweyn & wife Kara

Hosts at the annual Rune-Net Heathen Winter Feast

Made in the USA
Lexington, KY
23 November 2011